In Christ's Name

A Bible Study on Spiritual Growth

*Dear Jane,
May God bless
you in the service
Dellanna*

Larry M. Taylor

Dellanna O'Brien

Woman's Missionary Union
Birmingham, Alabama

Woman's Missionary Union
P. O. Box 830010
Birmingham, Alabama 35283-0010

Dewey Decimal Classification: 248.4
Subject Headings: SPIRITUAL LIFE—BIBLICAL TEACHING
                  CHRISTIAN LIFE
                  BIBLE—STUDY

Unless otherwise noted, Scripture quotations are from the Holy Bible, New International Version. Copyright © 1973, 1978, 1984 International Bible Society. Used by permission of Zondervan Bible Publishers.

Cover design by Janell E. Young

ISBN: 1-56309-074-0
W934108•0693•7.5M1

Introduction

At 13, Nick was worried because his friends were growing rapidly, while he had not yet begun to grow. He was the smallest boy in his class, and while all the other guys had hit their adolescent growth period, he still looked like a child. He complained to his parents about his problem. Finally, his father insisted he go to the family doctor.

The doctor found everything to be normal and told her young patient that he was perfectly healthy. Everyone is different. People come into their growth period at different ages. With these words the doctor did everything she could to reassure Nick.

Nick was relieved but not satisfied. He went home and talked with his dad, who said, "The doctor obviously sees nothing to be concerned about."

"Yes, but I still want to grow like my friends," Nick said.

"Well, son, if you can't grow just now the way you want to, maybe you could grow the way you *can* grow," his father advised.

"What do you mean?" Nick asked.

"There are many different kinds of growth," his dad explained. "Some are harder to see and measure than others. You've got a good mind, son. Perhaps you could concentrate on growing in your thinking. And you're a good tennis player. You could work to improve your game. You could do what you do best. That's a kind of growth."

And suddenly, Nick had something new to think about.

It's difficult to see how any Christian's faith can grow without serious and regular Bible study. Growth, after all, is what the Christian life is about. It's too late for innocence and far too early for perfection in any of us, but God is very much interested in our possibilities for growth.

Growth in the Christian's life gets translated along the way into service, missions, and ministry; growth is not merely for growth's sake. In the process of growth we are empowered, we are called and made accountable, we learn the servant model of ministry, and we receive an invitation to serve in Christ's name by getting involved in the needs of a crying and wounded world.

If we are to minister to a hurting world, we will need a power that is not our own. Section 1 in this book deals with power. We are empowered by the might of God as expressed through Christ and the Holy Spirit.

When we have been empowered by God, our calling and accountability come into focus. Section 2 explores this calling and accountability. Then we move to section 3, which gives us the great model of servanthood—Jesus as the Suffering Servant. Then, acceptance of servanthood opens the door to involvement, section 4.

In Christ's Name is designed to help you grow in these four areas. Larry Taylor has written the Bible studies; Dellanna O'Brien has provided the reflection section at the end of each chapter. Read with your Bible beside you. *In Christ's Name* uses the New International Version; you may have a favorite version to which you'd like to refer as you study. Also, keep close at hand a notebook and pen to jot down ideas and questions as they arise. You'll also want the notebook to write down your answers to the reflection questions.

The point of Bible study is growth. We can all grow, and while you may not be able just now to grow in all the ways you'd like, perhaps through *In Christ's Name* you'll be able to grow now in the ways you can. It's certainly something to think about.

Larry M. Taylor
Dellanna O'Brien

Section 1

Power

1

The Power of God

Focal passage: Jeremiah 32:6-17
Focal verse: Jeremiah 32:17

The theme for this section is Empowerment. The world today is obsessed with power—military power, political power, financial power—what has been called the arrogance of power. But we are concerned with a different kind of power—God's power for missions and witness. That is the kind of power you will be learning about in these chapters.

Finding Fresh Hope

Our focal passage is chapter 32 of Jeremiah's prophecy. Because Jeremiah's book is so intimate and revealing, he lets us know who he is. We know more about Jeremiah than any other figure in the Old Testament except David.

Jeremiah was born about 645 years before Christ, when Manassah was king of Judah. Jeremiah came from a priestly family, which provided him certain benefits, such as education and status, that served him well in his 40-year ministry. But Jeremiah also had personal gifts. He was an unusually sensitive and gifted man who could plumb great spiritual depths. He was eccentric, as were most of the prophets. But Jeremiah possessed enormous poetic gifts, and the moody temperament that often goes with such gifts. It's no accident that this man was remembered as the weeping prophet. No figure in the Bible except Jesus and Job knew more about suffering than Jeremiah.

Now a word about the background into which Jeremiah came. Manassah, the most wicked king in Judah's history, was little more than a puppet of Assyria. For more than 100 years Assyria had been the dominant empire; all other peoples, including Judah's, were subject to her. But now Assyria was declining and a new power was on the horizon. In 605 B.C., Babylon, rising from the east under Nebuchadnezzar, captured Judah. Seven years later, in 598 B.C., the first deportation of captives left Jerusalem for Babylon. It wasn't a large deportation—between 4,000 and 5,000 people probably. But the captives in this first deportation were the wealthiest people:artists—those skilled in stone masonry and various other arts; and the intellectuals—the cream of the crop.

Jerusalem itself was temporarily spared. Then, just 10 years later, in January of 588 B.C., Babylon sieged Jerusalem again, this time because of the king's rebellion against Nebuchadnezzar. This siege lasted for 18 months. At the end, Jerusalem fell. The people were deported in large numbers to Babylon, and Judah was wiped from the face of the earth. Darkness descended upon the nation of the Hebrews.

Our Bible study takes place in the final months of the kingdom of Judah. By late summer, 8 months after the siege began, the situation was desperate. All hope for deliverance was gone, food was scarce, and the Babylonian armies were just outside the walls.

Where was Jeremiah? In prison. Because he had continued to prophesy, because he had dared tell the king not to oppose the Babylonians any further, because he himself had tried to leave the city, he was in prison. Jeremiah's career was near its end and he was broken in health and spirit.

For 40 years Jeremiah had spoken the word of God to a people who were deaf to that word. Now his world was coming to an end. The Babylonian army at the gates of Jerusalem was in effect the nuclear bomb of Jeremiah's day.

In the middle of the prophecy of Jeremiah, chapters 30 through 33, is that portion of the book believed to focus on

Jeremiah's later years. These chapters are known as the little book of comfort. By chapter 30, you're ready for a little comfort. This prophet had known anguish and agony for 40 years, but late in his life he managed to break through to fresh hope. Our Bible study is about that hope.

Read the focal passage now. "Jeremiah said, 'The word of the Lord came to me: Hanamel, son of Shallum your uncle will come to you and say, "Buy my field which is at Anathoth, for the right of redemption by purchase is yours." '"

Jeremiah was in prison and a word came to him from the Lord saying, *You're going to have a visit from a cousin. He's going to come to you in prison and say, "Cousin, why don't you buy my field in our hometown of Anathoth, just three miles away from Jerusalem? After all, it belongs to you."*

This word was almost unbelievable. To be sure, Jeremiah felt that it must be a word from God. Time and time again God's word had come to him. Jeremiah had known what Nietzsche must have had in mind when he spoke of a "long obedience in the same direction."[1]

Do you know something about a long obedience in the same direction? Jeremiah had gone obediently in the same direction for 40 years and now a word came to him in a hopeless moment. But our God is never hopeless. God always has options. Roy Fairchild says, "Hope is imagining another way."[2] A word from God in an apparently desperate and hopeless situation began to create once more within Jeremiah fresh hope.

Hope always transcends optimism and pessimism. Jeremiah might be described as always optimistic about the future of God, but pessimistic about world history and human nature. Jeremiah knew that the heart is desperately wicked and unknown to us (Jer. 17:9), and that we can no more change our hearts than the leopard can change his spots (Jer. 13:23).

Have you ever noticed how people who are always optimistic can appear to be insensitive? Fairchild also says, "Hope is not optimism. Optimism tends to minimize the tragic sense of life."[3] Christians, of all people, should know something about the tragic sense of life. Modern secular optimism is the unrealistic product of an affluent, technological age, that has more money that it knows what to do with.[4]

But for Jeremiah, hope went beyond optimism and pessimism. The word that came from God contained a promise.

Symbols of Hope

The prophets loved symbolic acts. They named their children symbolic names, wore yokes on their shoulders, walked the streets of Jerusalem hardly dressed. They were fond of symbolic acts, but to Jeremiah at this moment this act surely seemed irrational, maybe even absurd. There's not much apparent hope in buying a farm which is at the moment being trampled under the feet of an invading army. But for 40 years this prophet had listened to a word from God. In hope against hope, Jeremiah struggled to believe.

Have you ever noticed that hope seems to come easier for some people than for others? Jeremiah had to struggle to believe. If you've taken the time to read his prophecy, you know that on every page, Jeremiah shares his doubts. He knew that faith without doubt is dead. Jeremiah knew that doubt can become the cutting edge of fresh new faith. Poet W. H. Auden said, "To choose what is difficult all one's days as if it were easy, that is faith."[5]

Just as God had promised, Hanamel came with the offer of the field.

Jeremiah says, "Then I knew that this was the word of the Lord" (Jer. 32:8b). Jeremiah's cousin confirmed for him what Jeremiah had already heard from the Lord. Don't you love to have what you think is God's word confirmed for you by someone? We need to confirm the word of the Lord for each other.

It's wonderful to know that Jesus loves me because the Bible tells me so. But I need to see the love of Jesus in someone's life as well. The love of Jesus takes on fresh incarnation whenever we confirm the word of the Lord for people in one of life's prisons.

In verses 9 and following the prophet swings into action. He'd been in prison; everything was desperate. Life was almost over. His spirit was broken, time was coming to an end, and there was no hope. Then the word of the Lord came to him. Notice beginning with verse 9 what happens to a prophet when the word of the Lord comes to him. Especially notice the verbs.

"'So I *bought* the field at Anathoth from my cousin Hanamel and *weighed* out for him seventeen shekels of silver. I *signed* and *sealed* the deed, had it witnessed, and *weighed* out the silver on the scales. I *took* the deed of purchase—the sealed copy containing the terms and conditions, as well as the unsealed copy—and I *gave* this deed to Baruch son of Neriah, the son of Mahseiah, in the presence of my cousin Hanamel and of the witnesses who *had signed* the deed of all the Jews *sitting* in the courtyard of the guard. In their presence I *gave* Baruch these instructions: "This is what the Lord Almighty, the God of Israel, says: *Take* these deeds, both the sealed and unsealed copies of the deed of purchase, and *put* them in a clay jar so they will last a long time"'" (Jer. 32:9-14; author's italics).

Aren't we glad he did that? "'For this is what the Lord God Almighty, the God of Israel, says: Houses, fields and vineyards will again be bought in this land'" (Jer. 32:15).

Can you imagine a better symbol of hope for a future that he himself would never see? In one of the most eloquent acts in the Scriptures, Jeremiah finally broke through to hope.

Someone once asked Martin Luther, the great reformer, what he would do if he knew that the end of the world would come tomorrow. Luther replied that he would plant a tree. Jeremiah answered the same question in effect by going out and buying a field.

In verse 16, Jeremiah does exactly what we would expect. When a word has come from God, what's a prophet to do but pray? "After I had given the deed of purchase to Baruch the son of Neriah, I prayed to the Lord: 'Ah, Sovereign Lord! You have made the heavens and the earth by your great power and outstretched arm. Nothing is too hard for you'" (Jer. 32:16-17).

Prayers are always the appropriate response to God. In Jeremiah's prayer he first addresses God the Creator (v. 17), the One Who has made the heavens and the earth.

In the following verses Jeremiah gives thanksgiving and praise for God's great acts. God shows steadfast love (v. 18);

He is great in counsel and mighty deeds (v. 19); and He shows signs and wonders (v. 20).

In verse 21 Jeremiah talks about God the Redeemer. "You brought your people Israel out of Egypt." The same God Who is God the Creator is also God the Redeemer. To redeem is to deliver. The One Who creates is the One Who delivers; the One Who delivers is the One Who has created. What the world needs now is a fresh vision of hope because people are anxious and desperate and the stakes in our world have never been higher. We live truly in apocalyptic times.

If hope is born out of hopelessness, could it be that power is born out of weakness? The power of God is best seen at life's extremities when human hope is gone and human resources are depleted, because then we are in the position to be open to a word from God—a promise of hope, a fresh lease on our mission. God's power is enough, and our confession of it is the same as Jeremiah's.

Ah, Lord God, it is thou who has made the heavens and the earth by thy great power. Nothing is too hard for thee (Jer. 32:17).

The Power of God

Talk about desperation!

In prison.

In the midst of famine.

Depleted of all resources.

The enemy at the gate.

Still Jeremiah prayed, believed, and acted. How was it possible for Jeremiah to retain hope in the midst of such desperate circumstances?

Walter and Kathryn were the model parents in their neighborhood and church. To outsiders it appeared they had everything going for them. That is, until their daughter Beth ran away from home the first time. Several years later, Walter and Kathryn are rearing the illegitimate, crack-addicted baby of their still wayward daughter.

Marsha married Glen when she was only 18. She was grateful to Glen for rescuing her from a miserable situation at home. How could she know that within a few years Glen would abandon her? Now, Marsha picks up the pieces and attempts to make a new life for herself and her children.

Just the Facts

While drug abuse has declined in the last decade, it is still the significant cause of almost all types of crime in our country. Alcohol is the drug of choice.[6] Babies are born daily with fetal alcohol syndrome or addicted to crack. Missing persons are often runaway teenagers, caught up in dope trafficking, prostitution, and other crimes.

Divorce affects millions in our nation. Additionally, one in four babies is born to an unmarried mother. It is predicted that half of all children today will spend some part of their childhood in a single-parent home.[7]

If these tragedies have touched you, either directly or indirectly, you are not alone. Few families have escaped the heartbreak of lives caught up in the world's deceitful web. Where is the hope for these people?

In your notebook list your personal concerns. Perhaps they seem insignificant compared to those recounted above. Maybe they are even more grievous! Whatever they are, write them down. No concern you have—regardless of how small or how great—is outside His care and note. List also your special concerns for others close to you.

Beyond the Facts

When facing difficult circumstances, we often forget the power of God to intervene. We try everything else to resolve our problems. God stands by, waiting for us to discover the futility of our own devices, before He suggests, "How about buying a field?" which being translated is, "How much do you really trust Me?"

Look again at your list of burdens. Give them to the loving God who "sees and knows all our infirmities." Nothing is too hard for Him!

In Spite of the Facts

Jeremiah bought a field. Martin Luther would have planted a tree. Marsha raises her children. These are not just responses to a difficult circumstance, but statements—statements that in events of all-consuming despair, there is hope. Jeremiah could have lashed out in anger at the people whose sins had caused his plight. Anyone could understand Marsha's resentment toward her husband. Each, however, has turned from blaming someone else to blessing God, through a tangible act, affirming that "nothing is too hard for God."

As you once again consider your own burdens, what can you do to demonstrate your hope that faith and love will prevail? Write down your possibilities and ask God to help you choose the ones you should act upon.

[1]Friedrich Nietzsche, in *Beyond Good and Evil,* as quoted by Eugene H. Peterson in *A Long Obedience in the Same Direction* (Downers Grove, IL: InterVarsity Press, 1980), 9.

[2]Roy W. Fairchild, Gammon Lecture Series, Fort Sanders Hospital, Knoxville, TN, May 1983. (Personal notes).

[3]Roy W. Fairchild, *Finding Hope Again* (New York: Harper and Row, 1980), 50-51.

[4]Ibid., 51.

[5]W. H. Auden, "For the Time Being," in *Collected Poems* (New York: Random House, Inc.,1976), 283.

[6]Bureau of the Census, *Statistical Abstract of the United States, 1992* (Washington, DC: Government Printing Office, 1992), 127.

[7]"New Families, Old Families," *The Futurist,* January-February 1993, vol. 27, no. 1, 45.

2

The Power of Christ

Focal passage: Mark 4:35 to 5:43
Focal verse: Mark 4:41

Jesus is constantly on the go in the Gospel of Mark. Consequently, Mark is interested in Jesus' miracles which He performed on His travels. We have in Mark's Gospel only a few fragments of Jesus' teaching, and no sermons. But no other Gospel gives such prominence to the miracles; in fact, the miracles occupy more than a quarter of this Gospel. These miracles show Christ as powerful Lord. This is probably by design because Mark was writing in and for the early church.

Early Christians had a long, intense struggle with the memory of Jesus' death by crucifixion. The cross was widely regarded as a death of weakness, a death for criminals. The cross was the most ignominious kind of execution. In the church, the memory of Jesus' miracles reminded these struggling Christians of the power Jesus demonstrated in His mighty deeds.

Lord over All

The focal passage is from the fourth and fifth chapters of Mark's Gospel, which form a unit of four miracle stories. Mark uses this cluster device to say something about Christ's power and compassion. These stories include lots of detail. Mark is good at that. And Mark shows us in these miracles the

13

powerful Son of God and constantly points us to faith in Him.

In this section are three themes: the theme of compassion, the theme of power, and the theme of faith. There is also a subtle, but deliberate, progression in the nature of these four miracles.

The first miracle shows Jesus in His power over nature (Mark 4:35-41). Jesus had been teaching all afternoon. He was weary, so, with His disciples, He left the crowd and they pushed off in a boat. The sea was at that moment calm and placid. But the Sea of Galilee is 600 feet below sea level, and subject to violent storms. No sooner were they out from the shore than the winds began to rise, the waves began to foam, and the storm reached its peak. The disciples were frightened, but Jesus was asleep. The storm did not wake Him at all. He was weary, but in complete calm, peace, and trust because He was in His Father's hands.

The disciples, fearing the waves and wind, went to the Master and shook Him. Waking Him, they said, "Don't you care?" They were panic-stricken, so they wanted to share their panic with Jesus.

Have you ever prayed that way? Have you ever gone to the Lord so full of panic and anxiety that you felt the least He could do was to get panicky along with you?

"Don't you even care?" the disciples asked Him. "Have you no sympathy for us?" The first theme comes into view, the theme of compassion and sympathy. The storm hadn't bothered Him in the least; the anxieties of His disciples did bother Him. The anxieties of His disciples always bothered Him.

So Jesus stood to His feet, and gazing toward the heavens, the wind blowing through His hair, the waves lapping over the sides of the boat, Jesus rebuked the storm, the winds, and waves. The verb in the Greek text means "he rapped the storm on the knuckles." He rapped the storm on the knuckles and said, "Be still, be calm." The seas obeyed Him instantly and returned to their placid, dull, green, silky surface.

Nature instantly obeyed because she recognized her Lord, that Word which was in the beginning, "through him all things were made; without him nothing was made that has been made" (John 1:1-3).

He turned to His disciples and said, "Do you still have no faith?" (Mark 4: 40). The second theme enters into these miracle units—the theme of faith. *Have you no faith? Did you not know that I was in the ship with you through the storm all along?*

Jesus' question was, "'Why are you so afraid? Do you still have no faith?' They were terrified and asked each other, 'Who is this? Even the wind and the waves obey him!'" (Mark 4:40-41).

The Gospel of Mark moves forward on a device called the Messianic secret. Mark is the only Gospel to use this device to any extent. In the Gospel of Mark, Jesus' identity is a secret, gradually revealed through the 16 chapters. Mark brings into focus through the disciples' question the central theme of his Gospel, the identity of Jesus. *Who then is this that even the storms, and the wind, and the sea—nature, obey Him?*

The question comes up again in the following chapters. The demons announce Jesus' identity for everybody to hear (Mark 3:11-12). At Caesarea Philippi Jesus will broach the subject with His disciples as they walk the roads and He says to them, "'Who do people say I am?' . . . 'But what about you?' he asked. 'Who do you say I am?'" (Mark 8:27,29). Peter had the answer, but he didn't have the proper understanding to go with it because he resisted the idea of a suffering Messiah. "'Get behind me, Satan!' he said. 'You do not have in mind the things of God, but the things of men'" (Mark 8:33).

In chapter 5, beginning with verse 1, we see Jesus' lordship expand. As He is Lord over nature, so He is also Lord over the demons. When they got to the other side of the lake they were in Gentile country. Jesus is always going back and forth across the sea in the Gospel of Mark. He shows Jesus going from the Jewish side of the lake, over to the Gentile side, and back to the Jewish side. And there is always a storm on the lake, a subtle way of saying that any time Christ tries to bring together these two ancient ways of thinking and living, Jewish and Gentile, expect storms.

When they landed on the shore, they were met by a man who lived in the tombs, a violent man possessed of demons (Mark 5:2-3). This man represents the most extreme example of demon possession in the New Testament. This was a sinister place. This was a sinister man. Behind them was a stormy and sinister sea. Mark has skillfully prepared us to meet a man who has a storm within himself, by bringing us over a sea that is also stormy.

Everything is violent, dangerous. This man had been chained many times by the local citizens, but he had broken the chains. Perhaps it had not entered anyone's mind in years to try any kind of therapy on him but chains.

The disciples were terrified and started to inch back toward the boat. But Jesus was fearless and perfectly calm; instantly the demons recognized Him. The disciples hadn't quite figured it out yet. *Who is this man that even the wind and the storms obey Him?*

But the demons knew Him. "What do you want with me, Jesus, Son of the Most High God?" they asked (Mark 5:7). In the Gospel of Mark the demons serve as loudspeakers, and apparently Jesus' first attempt at casting out these demons was unsuccessful (Mark 5:8).

Jesus backed up and took a different approach to this demon-filled man. He said to him, "What is your name?" (Mark 5: 9). To give your name was to give yourself.

My name, the man may have thought. *My name. Who am I?* "'My name is Legion,' he replied, 'for we are many'" (Mark 5: 9). I can still hear Professor Quick back at Ouachita Baptist University in sociology class saying, "Knowledge begins with the naming of a thing."[1]

What is your name? Can you name the demons within you? There is no hope of their being exorcised until they can be named.

The demons knew what was about to happen; they were frightened. They begged Jesus not to disembody them, not to bring them into the full light of day. Demons don't like the light. They don't like to be disembodied. Nearby was a herd of swine; they begged Jesus to send them there. Jesus permitted it to happen and the swine, now full of the devil, thrashed about and then in unison followed their leader down a steep hill to their death in the sea (Mark 5:11-13).

Were the swineherders disturbed! They saw this year's

profit, next year's profit, the profit of the year after that going into the sea. They fled into the nearby Gentile city to tell what had happened. The whole population turned out to see such a thing, and when they got there, what did they see? They saw a man, formerly deranged, demonic, violent, now clothed and in his right mind, sitting at the feet of Jesus listening and talking.

What did these people from the nearby city do? They begged Jesus to leave (Mark 5:17). Jesus was bad for business.

As far as we know, He honored their request and never came back to their shores. These people feared sanity more than insanity, change more than disease. Lots of people say they would like to change, but most folks don't really want to change. John Henry Newman said, "In a higher world it is otherwise, but here below to live is to change, and to be perfect is to have changed often."[2]

This man had been dramatically changed. Now when you are changed like that, what do you want to do? You want to be a missionary. So did he. He asked Jesus for the privilege of going with Him as part of His entourage so that he might witness every place he went (Mark 5:18).

Jesus said, "'Go home to your family and tell them how much the Lord has done for you, and how he has had mercy on you'" (Mark 5:19). And what has Mark said to us? Jesus is Lord over demons.

But Mark isn't through with us. Nor is Jesus. In the verses that follow, he is about to make the point that Jesus is also Lord over disease (Mark 5:21-34). They got back into the boat; crossed the lake again to the Jewish side, where they were met by a crowd of people, among them one Jairus, ruler of a synagogue. Jairus was a layman. He had been elected the president of his synagogue. He was a thoroughly orthodox Jewish man; he was also blessed by God with an open mind. Thank God for open minds!

But, said William Temple, the late archbishop of Canterbury, "The purpose of an open mind is to close it on something." Jairus was ready to close on Jesus as the last, best hope for the healing of his little girl who was sick and at the point of death.

He asked Jesus to come with him to the house, lay His hands on her, and heal her. Jesus, Jairus, and the entourage of disciples and curiosity seekers started off toward Jairus' house. En route the crowd grew to a multitude, and suddenly Jesus stopped.

Here Mark resorts to one of the most interesting devices in his Gospel. It's called a sandwich. He gives us a story within a story. A sandwich, you know, has a layer of bread, and then some meat and goodies in between, and then another layer of bread. Mark uses this sandwich approach, according to Professor James Blevins, some dozen times in his Gospel.[3] Here he is giving a miracle within a miracle, a story within a story, a kind of sandwich as it were.

Jesus stopped suddenly and said, "Who touched my clothes?" (Mark 5:30).

Who touched you, Lord? People are thronging around you. Why do you ask who touched me?

No, somebody touched me with meaning, with faith. Who was it?

Humbly, greatly embarrassed, a woman stepped forward and began to tell her story. Look in verse 26 at what Mark tells about this woman.

This is Mark's comment on the medical profession of his day. This woman had suffered much under many physicians. She had spent all she had and she was no better. But in faith, some might say superstition, she believed that if she could just touch the garments of this man about whom she had heard, she might be healed. So she had, and instantly felt herself made well.

At the same instant, Jesus felt power go out and stopped to inquire. Here the power theme comes into play. The woman humbly came forward, fell to her knees before Jesus and told Him the whole truth.

Isn't it marvelous to fall on our knees before Jesus and just tell Him the whole truth, the whole story of our individual sickness?

Jesus said to her, "'Daughter, your faith has healed you. Go in peace and be freed from your suffering'" (Mark 5:34).

Jesus had no sooner ceased talking about faith than came

servants from Jairus' household to say, "'Your daughter is dead,' they said. 'Why bother the teacher any more?'" (Mark 5:35).

Jesus ignored the report completely and said, "'Don't be afraid; just believe'" (Mark 5:36). Coming from anyone else that would sound calloused, but Jesus knew the art of ignoring. The art of ignoring false reports is one of the finest of all the Christian arts. Why did Jesus know how to ignore this report? Jesus knew that God always has the last word; even death itself is subject to His power. And so He said, don't be afraid, just believe.

They proceeded toward Jairus' home. "He did not let anyone follow him except Peter, James, and John the brother of James" (Mark 5:37).

They went on to the house, where the funeral was already in full procession. Professional mourners had been hired and they were wailing and screeching. Jesus heard them long before they got to the house. "He went in and said to them, 'Why all this commotion and wailing? The child is not dead but asleep.' But they laughed at him" (Mark 5:39). They laughed Him to scorn. *What do you mean, only sleeping?*

Jesus cleared the house. He reached over and touched this little girl by the hand and said to her, "'Little girl, I say to you, get up!'" (Mark 5:41). And she arose. This is the only one of Jesus' resurrection miracles that is recorded in all three of the synoptic Gospels, Matthew, Mark and Luke. Resurrection is forever the central miracle of the Bible. In the final verse Jesus said to them, "He gave strict orders not to let anyone know about this" (Mark 5:43). Mark's Messianic secret again comes into play. *Don't tell anybody what's happened. It's not time yet for everybody to know Who I am and what I can do.*

Where We Are Going

So what do we have in these four miracle stories? We have a lesson in Jesus' sympathy because the miracles move from the impersonal to the personal. Nature is rather impersonal, but He stills the storms, the winds, and the waves. A demonic man is only half a man. A woman with a long illness is a very personal need. A little girl who has died and a father who is in grief are surely the most personal need.

There's a progression as we see Jesus' sympathy unfold. We have a lesson on Jesus' power. He's Lord over nature, over demons, over disease. He's Lord even over death.

If he is Lord over all of these things, what's left to fear?

Here we are taught something about faith, because faith is the means of appropriating the power of Christ. In the ship Jesus said to the disciples, "Where is your faith?" To the woman now healed, He said, "'Daughter, your faith has healed you. Go in peace and be freed from your suffering'" (Mark 5:34).

There is no phenomenon in nature, in man, nor in woman over which Christ is not fully the Lord, because He has power over nature, over devils, over disease, and even over death.

Doesn't something have to die before something new can be born? We love Easter and its resurrection, but we don't like Good Friday and its deaths. But something always has to die before something new can be born. Just now death wails are being heard all over the land, all over the world. Above the funeral wails already keening in our ears, let's not fail to hear another word, a word from the Lord. "See, I am doing a new thing! Now it springs up; do you not perceive it?" (Isa. 43:19). Do we not perceive it? Our God is the God who always is doing new things. His Christ has all the power we will ever need. We tap that power by faith because Christ is our way into an uncertain future.

The Power of Christ

How much power is evident in your life? Can you handle a threatening storm? Can you deal with the legion of demands and stresses of your life? Have you, like the woman who approached Jesus, suffered a great deal under the care of many doctors and spent all you have, but there is no healing? Have you faced the death of a loved one?

What enables a Christian to cope in the midst of any crisis? How is it possible not only to bear the load but to use the experience to strengthen the spiritual life?

Just the Facts

Live long enough and storms will come. No one is exempt from the troubles of life. The disciples did everything they were trained as experienced fishermen to do, yet the raging storm continued to threaten their very lives. Out of desperation, they furiously, but unsuccessfully, fought the elements, while with a word, the Master stilled the tempest. In the storms of life, struggle is often counterproductive. *Fear not; let go and let God*—good advice for us.

Perhaps even now the most productive action you can take is to relax in the power and love of the Master. He desires to bring you to safety through whatever storm you may be encountering.

Beyond the Facts

Remember the burdens you listed in chapter 1? Look at them again. They are the storms in your own life. Whether created through an act of nature, the onslaught of evil forces, or developed through your own humanity, Christ's message to you is, *Peace, be still. The Master Pilot is in control.*

Christ's power goes through every storm, every threat, every infirmity, straight to the heart of the person in its grip. Fear not.

Jesus knows all your difficulties and He cares about you. While storms within and storms without may catch you in their grip, the Master is all powerful; He hears the plea,

> Don't you care?
> My name is Legion; for we are many.
> I only wanted to touch the hem of your garment.
> Heal my child.

Pray right now Paul's own confession of dependence upon the power of Jesus: "I can do everything through him who gives me strength" (Phil. 4:13).

In Spite of the Facts

James wrote to the early Christians:

> Consider it pure joy, my brothers, when you face trials of many kinds, because you know that the testing of your faith develops perseverance. Perseverance must finish its work so that you may be mature and complete, not lacking anything (James 1:2-4).

Never again would the disciples experience a storm without remembering the instant calm resulting from the Master's, *Peace, be still*. The former demoniac's testimony to others caught in the grip of evil power must have begun something like this: *Let me tell you about the time Jesus delivered me from death in the tombs*. The woman who received healing just by touching Christ's garment must have constantly testified to His power over the flesh. Jairus could never look at his precious child again without remembering the One Who gave her back to him.

What demons did you name when you read of the Gadarene demoniac? (pp. 15-17) How have you experienced Christ's power over them?

What happens when you try to struggle against your personal storms instead of relying on Jesus?

Record your answers in your notebook.

The completion of the saga of deliverance comes only in sharing it with others. Think of a personal storm Jesus stilled. In your notebook, write your experience. Compose a psalm of praise to Jesus for His power over your life's storms.

Tell someone today of His power in your life. Perhaps, your words of hope will bring confidence to one who is even now in the midst of a raging storm.

---

[1]Randy Quick, Ouachita Baptist University, Arkadelphia, Arkansas.

[2]John Henry C. Newman, *The Development of Christian Doctrine* (New York: Longman's, Green, and Co., 1949), 37-38; as quoted by Ernest T. Campbell, *Christian Manifesto* (New York: Harper and Row, 1970), 92.

[3]James Blevins, presentation to the National Seminar on Preaching, Southern Baptist Theological Seminary, March 1990.

3

The Power of the Holy Spirit

Focal passage: Romans 8:26-27
Focal verse: Romans 8:26

The subject of the focal passage, obviously, is the Spirit. The Spirit is mentioned 4 times in verses 26 and 27. In fact, the Spirit is the subject of the entire eighth chapter of Romans. This emphasis on the Spirit is in the sharpest possible contrast to what Paul has said about the law in chapter 7. Later on, you might want to read chapter 7 to find 22 references to the law. Paul follows that with chapter 8 where there are 18 references to the Spirit.

Prayer is one of the most universal experiences of the Christian life. Every Christian prays, to some extent or another, but I'm convinced that most of us are amateurs at prayer. Prayer is a foreign land that we visit as tourists. When we come back, we discover we cannot adequately share with others the experiences we had there.

I once visited Coventry Cathedral while in England doing a pulpit exchange. I had heard about Coventry and I went to see what others had seen and had been unable to describe. The old fourteenth-century cathedral, bombed in World War

II, still sits there. Everything was blown away from its foundations except the shell of the old cathedral. Beside it they've built a new, modern cathedral, unmistakably twentieth-century. The two of them stand side by side, as a reminder forever. The theme of the entire complex is forgiveness.

I came back home and tried to tell my congregation about that experience, only to discover that words were not adequate. That was an experience in a dimension beyond words.

Paul's words in Romans 8:26-27 seem mysterious to us. He says that prayer is a human impossibility, yet we need to pray, because our spirit must commune with God's Spirit. We might say that prayer is the impossible possibility on which our very spiritual lives depends, because without prayer we have no power.

We Do Not Know How to Pray As We Ought

In these two verses Paul has some good news and some bad news. First he gives the bad news. The gospel is always bad news before it's good news.[1] It's the bad news about our littleness. It's the bad news about our weakness, our sin, our helplessness, and our powerlessness.

So, here is Paul's bad news. *We do not know how to pray as we ought.* Now we can fill in the blanks for ourselves, endlessly, I suppose. We don't know how to pray as we ought because we are weak. We are powerless, and Jesus told His disciples in John 15:5, "Apart from me you can do nothing."

We don't know how to pray as we ought because our knowledge is limited. Never forget that. Humility becomes us. How often do we claim to know more than we really know? Paul reminds us, "Now we see but a poor reflection as in a mirror; then we shall see face to face. Now I know in part; then I shall know fully, even as I am fully known" (1 Cor. 13:12). Even our knowledge of self is limited. We don't know how to pray as we ought, because we don't really know our own needs. Like children, we ask for things that would only hurt us if we received them. We don't even understand our own complexity—body, mind, and spirit.

We don't know the purposes of God, what Dorothy Sayers calls the "mind of the maker."[2] We don't know how to pray as we ought because we can't see the future. Life can change forever with the ring of the telephone.

We don't know how to pray as we ought, because we are hung up on words. Words are conscious, left-brain tools, but prayer must rise from deeper levels. Sometimes we are frustrated because we live much deeper than we can speak.

Something happens in real prayer that can never be expressed in mere words. We limit ourselves to the verbal and the conversational in prayer, but there are so many ways of praying. Silence can be prayer. And meditation. And contemplation. We have let these spiritual disciplines go to our friends representing eastern religions and we have lost sight of the fact that our Christian tradition in silence and meditation and contemplation is deep and long.

During that pulpit exchange in England I got to the church to meet the organist before the first Sunday. He was a proper gentleman, tall, gray-haired, and distinguished. Throughout the weeks that followed I got to know him and we had several conversations. Late in the month he confided that his wife had been ill for a long time and that he could no longer pray. He felt the words just went nowhere.

I said to him, "What do you do that gives you genuine pleasure and soul satisfaction?"

He smiled and said, "Oh, at the keyboard! I can sit at my keyboard and play forever, and feel God close."

I said to him, "Then if you cannot pray as you would like, let your prayers come through your fingers and offer them up to God and call it your prayer."

How many ways can we pray beyond the verbal? Words are only marginal to the deep of the Spirit. Here is the bad news. We don't know how to pray as we ought. We'll not be able to hear the good news that Paul has in this passage until we fully listen to this bad news first.

What is the bad news? That prayer is a human impossibility, because all human efforts at prayer start with self and end with self. And that is nothing more than internal conversation.

The Spirit Helps Our Weakness

Now some good news!

"The Spirit helps us in our weakness" (Rom 8:26). The Spirit intercedes with God for us, not with mere words, but with sighs and groanings, too deep for words. The Spirit knows the language of God—it's the language of sighs and groanings. What words can never accomplish, the sighs of the Spirit do for us. One Who knows us better than we know ourselves prays in our behalf.

Have you ever come to the moment of prayer, only to discover that all you could get out was "Aah"? You're close to prayer at that moment. The Spirit is beginning to work. The conversation between the Holy Spirit within us and God the Father is so close that dialogue between them becomes wordless.

T. S. Eliot said poetry is an "ever new raid on the inarticulate."[3] Not a bad definition of prayer, for we can't articulate what we want. What does that mean for us? What does it mean that the Spirit intercedes with God the Father on our behalf? It means that the initiative in praying in the Spirit is always God's. Prayer begins with God, not with us. God makes the first move. God says the first word. Isn't it always so?

Creation was God's first move. We merely responded to it. He inaugurated a covenant with one family, one nation. They merely responded. His Son came in the flesh, God with us, Immanuel, and we have responded to Him.

As a child in Sunday School the first song I learned was "Jesus Loves Me." But the second song that I learned was "Oh, How I Love Jesus," which begins, "Oh, how I love Jesus, because He first loved me." He always makes the first move.

Prayer in the Spirit is God incarnate appealing to God transcendent. This idea of God interceding for us before Himself, if taken and pressed literally, becomes almost ridiculous, and yet it is in fact a symbol both genuine and profound. It reminds us that God knows more about us than we know about ourselves, and that God can represent us before the throne of grace because He knows the language.

Praying in the Spirit identifies God as subject, never as object. God is the eternal subject and that means we can't hold Him at arms length. We cannot hold God at examinable distance. God will be with us. We can only participate in the Spirit in that rich dialogue that is going on constantly between Father, and Son, and Holy Spirit.

We don't search for God as though He were an object to be found. Our search for Him is itself a testimony that He has already found us. In prayer we are talking with the ground of our being, the One Who is closer to us than hands or feet.

Roy Fairchild talks about some childish images of prayer we have. He calls one of them "the *Telestar* model." God is the great *Telestar* satellite, off in the sky, and we beam our requests off Him thinking that perhaps He'll answer us. You can probably think of other childish images.

"Prayer," says Roy Fairchild, "is paying loving attention to God, not off there somewhere, but within ourself."[4]

The Holy Spirit helps us to see things right. He gives us a new perspective, and so we sing "Open My Eyes, That I May See." We don't always see. We don't see because we've put out our own eyes. We've blinded ourselves in so many ways, living in this technological, empirical, and scientific age. We have decided, in advance, that miracles don't happen, that the world is only rational, that God never does interrupt the chain of cause and effect. We've put out our own eyes.

There is no completely innocent eye; we see what we want to see. The observing eye always shapes what it sees. The only thing in the world that is truly objective is an object. Once I take that object in and pass it through my mental filter and interpret its meaning, it is no longer the same. The Holy Spirit within us gives us eyes to see, gives us the right perspective, gives us what Paul calls, "the mind of the Spirit" (Rom.8:27).

Praying in the Spirit sensitizes us and enables us to see things whole where everything touches everything. And when prayer opens us up to see things whole, what do we start to see? We see that sure enough the kingdom is within us just as Jesus says, and the journey inward becomes the appropriate response to praying in the Spirit. Depth, rather than height, becomes the locale of God. And prayer is a loving conversation between God within us and God above us that has as its subject our well-being.

William Blake wrote:

There is a Moment in each Day that Satan cannot find,
Nor can his Watch Fiends find it; but the Industrious find
This Moment & it multiply, & when it once is found
It renovates every Moment of the Day if rightly placed."[5]

Have you found that moment? When we find that moment, it need never be said of us, "They have no power!"

The Power of the Holy Spirit

When you think of prayer, what comes to your mind? A beautifully articulated petition from your church's saint, a meeting for good Christians to attend, a little child's verse quoted at mealtime?

Henri Nouwen quotes a Russian mystic in what he calls "the best formulation of the prayer of the heart":

"To pray is to descend with the mind into the heart,
and there to stand before the face of the Lord
ever-present, all-seeing, within you."—Theophan the Recluse.[6]

Paul suggests, "We do not know what we ought to pray for, but the Spirit himself intercedes for us with groans that words cannot express" (Rom. 8:26).

So, there you have it. Definitions of prayer from two experts, and not one suggestion that the words are more important than the spirit.

Just the Facts

While few Christians would deny that prayer is important, few actually take the time to pray regularly. In an important study of religion in the US in 1989, Gallup and Castelli found that while there was an "enduring popularity" of religion, there was a significant gap between Americans' expressed beliefs and the state of the society they shape. In their research it was discovered that 51 percent of men and 69 percent of women say prayer is very important to them.[7]

Henry Blackaby notes, however: "I hear many persons say, 'I really struggle trying to have that (quiet) time alone with God.' If that is a problem you face, let me suggest something to you. Make the priority in your life to come to love Him with all your heart. That will solve most of your problem with your quiet time."[8]

Some people don't pray because they feel they don't know how. They are concerned that their prayers aren't formal enough, not beautiful enough, and not lengthy enough. Sometimes the briefest verbal prayers are the most powerful. John Bunyan has said, "In prayer it is better to have a heart without words, than words without a heart."[9]

Some years ago, James Flamming rushed to the home where the teenaged son had just been killed in an automobile accident. Going immediately to the parents, he took them both in his arms and moaned audibly for several seconds. What a beautiful demonstration of the groaning of the Spirit in the absence of meaningful words!

Beyond the Facts

The first step in learning to pray is presenting oneself to the Father, open, listening, expectant. Select a quiet place and time; ask Him to come to you; and wait upon Him. If you feel led to speak, know that it's the Spirit nudging you to pray. If not, just sit or kneel and enjoy the presence of the Father. Rely upon the Spirit within you to communicate your deepest thoughts. In time, your persistence and faithfulness will result in a natural flow of praise and adoration. You will long to seek His will and to intercede for others. Fellowship with the Father takes time, but it is infinitely worth the time invested.

In Spite of the Facts

The fact is, the world just goes too fast! It may be your best intention to set aside a few minutes for your quiet time, but before you know it, the time has disappeared.

Even when the time has been found, unbidden thoughts intrude, making concentration difficult. John Donne long ago confessed, "I throw myself down in my chamber, and I call in and invite God and His angels thither, and when they are there, I neglect God and His angels, for the noise of a fly, for the rattling of a coach, for the whining of a door."[10]

Every Christian has experienced these frustrations. Remember, however, that anything worthwhile must be pursued. Maintain that time when you are least likely to be interrupted, and hold to it. Return as quickly as possible to your prayers after dismissing unwanted thoughts. Remember, too, an interruption is not always bad. Sometimes it is God at work answering your prayers.

Write in your notebook the days in which you maintain a quiet time with God. How did the Holy Spirit speak to you?

What do you think of Larry Taylor's statement (p. 23) that most people are "amateurs at prayer"?

---

[1] Frederick Buechner, *Telling the Truth: The Gospel as Tragedy, Comedy, and Fairy Tale* (San Francisco: Harper and Row, 1977), 17, 70.

[2] Dorothy L. Sayers, *The Mind of the Maker* (New York: Meridian Books).

[3] T. S. Eliot, as quoted by Joseph Sittler, *The Anguish of Preaching* (Philadelphia: Fortress Press, 1966), 51.

[4] Roy Fairchild, Gammon Lecture Series, Fort Sanders Hospital, Knoxville, TN, May 1983.

[5] William Blake, "Milton," in *The Complete Poetry and Selected Prose of John Donne and the Complete Poetry of William Blake* (New York: Modern Library, 1941), 883.

[6] Henri Nouwen, *The Way of the Heart* (New York: Ballantine Books, 1981), 59.

[7] George Gallup, Jr., and Jim Castelli, *The People's Religion* (New York: Macmillan, 1989), 50.

[8] Henry Blackaby, *Experiencing God* (Nashville: Baptist Sunday School Board, 1990), 49.

[9] Albert M. Wells, Jr. ed. *Inspiring Quotations* (Nashville: Thomas Nelson Publishers, 1988), 158.

[10] John Donne, *Sermons*, no. 80.

4

Power for Witness

Focal passage: Acts 1:6-11
Focal verse: Acts 1:8

The book of Acts is Holy Ghost territory. Acts is uniquely the book of the Holy Spirit. We call this book the Acts of the Apostles out of long tradition. But it might better be called the "Acts of the Holy Spirit" because the Holy Spirit is the central figure, mentioned 56 times.

Asking the Wrong Question

In verse 6, the disciples had a question. "So when they met together, they asked him, 'Lord, are you at this time going to restore the kingdom to Israel?'"

Their question would suggest that nothing much had changed for them, even after the Resurrection. Their question is basically the same as their assumption just before the Crucifixion and the Resurrection (Luke 19:11). Their concept of the kingdom was still narrow, nationalistic, materialistic. They were still operating from limited hope and limited scope. To their minds the kingdom was still Israel.

The book of Acts is the story of how Jesus' disciples got free of their limited vision, and how Christians overcame their spiritual provincialism. For that reason Acts is ever new and fresh because in every generation we must overcome spiritual provincialism.

This passage begins with a question from the disciples. Unfortunately, it's the wrong question. There's certainly nothing wrong with questions. The Bible is a book of questions. "Am I my brother's keeper?" "If a man dies, shall he live again?" "Who is my neighbor?" "Why do the wicked prosper?" "How can they hear without a preacher?"

The Bible is a book of great questions. Jesus even asked why God had forsaken Him. The writer of Scripture, fully inspired by the Holy Spirit, felt no need to delete that from his text. So there's no reason for us to fear questions.

But here the disciples asked the wrong question. *Lord, are you ready now at last to restore the kingdom to Israel?* Jesus gave them a short answer. He said, "'It is not for you to know the times or dates the Father has set by his own authority.'" That was hardly the answer they expected. Jesus didn't denigrate their hope for the kingdom, but He did reject the idea of putting any time schedule on it.

What Jesus had to give His disciples was not more knowledge but more assurance. We are to be sustained not by the knowledge of things that can be known only to God, but by something else. In verse 8 Jesus is getting ready to name that something else.

These disciples hadn't yet understood that they themselves were the kingdom. Nor had they understood that they were to become the instruments through which that kingdom expands in an ever widening circle to embrace all mankind. It takes a lot of power to fuel the kingdom, and the disciples hadn't yet been connected to the power source.

Power and the Spirit

The disciples were at a point where they needed to hush, listen, and be connected with the power source. Jesus was ready for that. "'But you will receive power when the Holy Spirit comes on you; and you will be my witnesses in Jerusalem, and in all Judea and Samaria, and to the ends of the earth'" (Acts 1:8). Here are a promise of power, a gift of Holy Spirit, and a mission. Three things are in this verse: power, Holy Spirit, and an assignment—a mission.

Have you ever stopped to think that our faith is based entirely on promises? The promissory nature of the Christian faith is such that the people of God are always looking to the future. The Bible constantly points to the future, asking God's people to stand on the promises and to scan the horizon for fulfillment of those promises.

In verse 8 the promise is for power. The word used here for power is an interesting Greek term, *dunameis,* from which we get our English word *dynamic. And ye shall receive* dynamic. The word occurs in the New Testament 77 times.

There is another word for power, *exousia,* and it occurs 66 times, including verse 7. *Which the Father has fixed by his own* exousia. But in verse 8 another word for power is used, *dunameis*—the more common of the two words in the New Testament. *Dunameis* means actual power. It refers to miraculous power, while *exousia* refers to authority. They both can be translated power. *Dunameis* is an inherent, constant-flowing possession of power. In Luke's writings it's the energy of the Spirit.

In the book of Acts, this power, this dynamic, is always closely related to the Holy Spirit. In the writings of Luke this power is usually conceived in some kind of physical way. For instance, at the Lord's baptism in the Gospel of Luke there is the imagery of the dove descending. In the book of Acts, when the Holy Spirit finally does come in chapter 2, there are all kinds of physical evidence—the rush of mighty wind, tongues of fire, ecstatic speaking, and inspired preaching.

The purpose of all this power in the gift of the Holy Spirit is so that witness can take place. "'But you will receive power when the Holy Spirit comes on you,'" Jesus said (Acts 1:8).

Witness is one of Luke's favorite terms in the book of Acts. If someday you are shut in on a rainy afternoon and want to do an interesting biblical word study, go through the book of Acts and note all of the times *witness* is mentioned. The term occurs 21 times, either in noun or verbal form. Originally it was a legal term referring to bearing witness to the facts in a court of law, but in the book of Acts it came to mean witnessing to the facts about Christ and giving testimony to His power.

Luke combines witness to the facts and evangelistic confes-

sion, which is what we have in all of the New Testament—
fact plus confession, fact plus testimony, what the Lord has
done and what it means to someone.

This word *witness* is an interesting word. It is the Greek
word *martureo*, from which we get our English word *martyr*—
a solemn reminder of what witnessing sometimes cost in
those early centuries and still does today in some places.

Jesus doesn't leave witnessing to chance or imagination.
The book of Acts traces the spread of the gospel. Verse 8 does
it by way of preview, and it shows the spread of the gospel in
an ever-widening circle. The geographical scope starts at
home in Jerusalem, but soon expands to the ends of the earth.

In verse 6 the disciples have just asked a question about
the kingdom. But they limited their question to Israel.
Richard Halverson says, "The extrovert God of John 3:16 does
not begat an introvert people."[1] Jesus now said to them, *The
kingdom will be yours when you've witnessed to the ends of the
earth.* He called on them to have a wider vision, a bigger
dream, and a greater God.

Our dream for missions will never be any greater than our
vision of God. Until the heart is wide and the soul is high we
always occupy small spaces.

Ascension to God

In verse 9 Luke describes the Ascension. He is the only
Gospel writer to do so, and he describes it twice—once at the
end of his Gospel and now a second time at the beginning of
Acts. The Ascension itself is referred to in other New Testament writings in different ways. Sometimes it's called "to take
up," sometimes "to exalt," sometimes "to sit down at the right
hand of God," as in Ephesians 1:20.

"And when he had said this as they were looking on, he
was lifted up and a cloud took him out of their sight" (Acts
1:4). Luke seems to conceive of the Ascension as an event of
great significance located between the Resurrection and Pentecost. The Ascension brings closure to something so that the
story can continue in a new dimension. The Ascension's theological meaning is usually overlooked.

The Ascension, first, is an enacted symbol of the end of

Jesus' physical appearance to His disciples. The Ascension is dramatic. Have you ever stopped to think about Jesus' love for drama? Jesus told parables, but He also enacted parables, as when He made a clay out of spit and dust and put it on the eyes of a blind man.

Jesus told parables, Jesus enacted parables, but in a fuller and bigger sense Jesus was a parable.[2] He was the parable of God. Here we have an enacted symbol of the end of His physical appearances.

Second, the Ascension signals a new mode of existence and activity for Jesus.

In the Paraclete sayings of the Gospel of John, in chapters 14 through 17, the Holy Spirit is actually another Jesus. Someone has said when the Holy Spirit comes, we have new dimensions in our lives. Christ makes the Spirit concrete and the Spirit makes Christ universal. So a new mode was now being opened up.

Third, the Ascension denotes Jesus' exaltation to the position of power that is sometimes referred to in the Scriptures as the right hand of God (Acts 2:33). Jesus is assuming universal power; He is returning to the power source.

Fourth, the Ascension is a counterpart to the Incarnation. What happens in the Incarnation? God becomes man and comes down to dwell among us. What happens in the Ascension? The God-Man leaves us and goes back to God. Here we have two beautiful movements. Luke is the writer who gives the lovely account of the virgin birth in the opening chapters of his gospel. Just as he does that in the opening chapters of Luke, here in the opening chapters of Acts he gives act two, the Ascension, the return. The Gospel of John does it another way. In the first half of the Gospel of John the Son of man descends to the earth. Beginning with chapter 13 the Son of man ascends back to the Father. It's the same kind of motion.

Fifth, the Ascension is an offering to God of that perfect humanity which was crucified sacrificially. It consummates the salvation event by which God and believers are fully reconciled. When Jesus ascends to the Father, suddenly there is something new in the presence of God that never was there before—humanity.

The Ascension also means that we live in a new period, the period of mission. Between the times of Jesus' two appearances we live perennially between advents.

A Question and a Promise

In Acts 1:10 Luke writes, *And while they were gazing into heaven.* Luke loves this word *gazing.* Can't you just see them? Jesus has disappeared, but they are still looking into heaven.

"They were looking intently up into the sky as he was going, when suddenly two men dressed in white stood beside them" (perhaps the same two men mentioned in Luke 24), and they appear with a question. So many of the great questions of the New Testament are built around Jesus. There is the great question when the angel Gabriel comes to Mary to make the announcement, and Mary asks for all of us and for all times the question of Christmas, "How will this be?" (Luke 1:34). There's the great question of Resurrection asked at the tomb on Easter morning, "Why do you look for the living among the dead?" (Luke 24:5). Here we have the great question of the Ascension, *Why do you stand gazing into heaven?* (Acts 1:11).

Why do you suppose we do that? It's important to have these spiritual mountaintop moments to gaze into heaven, but, why do we continue to stand gazing into heaven? There's work to do. There's mission to perform. *Furthermore, this Jesus, Who was taken up from you into heaven, will come in the same way that you saw Him go into heaven* (Acts 1:11).

Here we have the fourth and final beautiful promise in these verses. Just look at these promises: verse 7, God will establish the kingdom; verse 8, power for mission must be received and can be; verse 8, it's the Holy Spirit that brings this power; and verse 11, Jesus is going to come back again.

So our passage opens with a question and ends with a question. It opens with the wrong question, *Lord, are you ready to give the kingdom back to Israel now?* It closes with the right question, *How long and why do you stand gazing into heaven when there's so much to do?*

Power for Witness

Whenever a family takes a car trip, one question is sure to arise from the children, perhaps not just once but many times: "How much longer before we get there?" The creative parent will find many variations of the response: "We still have a long way to go."

The apostles were concerned about the journey's conclusion. If Jesus had answered their *when* question about His Kingdom, the next inquiry would probably have been *how?*

Today many still have a preoccupation with the wrong questions. In Korea, a heretical sect led by prophet Lee Jang-nim, was told that Christ was coming on October 28, 1992. Because of the trauma this announcement created in the hearts and minds of followers who didn't know the Scriptures, several people committed suicide. Missionary Tom Daniel reported, "Now mockers will make it difficult for Koreans to turn to Christ, blaming God for not coming on man's schedule."[3]

Just the Facts

While there is always a great deal of interest surrounding Christ's Second Coming, Jesus would say to us, "It is not for you to know the details." As a friend of mine says, "I know Jesus is coming again; He just didn't put me on the planning committee!"

Jesus would also remind us, however: "We still have a long way to go before the journey is over."

When Jesus defined the scope of His kingdom, from Jerusalem to the ends of the earth, the apostles were no doubt overwhelmed. Jerusalem and Judea they knew, and even parts of Samaria, but to the ends of the earth? No wonder they stood gazing up into heaven. *Jesus, you mean we have to go to all those places before your kingdom is established?*

As demanding as the task seemed to the apostles, they had no clue as to the actual size and diversity of their world. At that very moment American Indians were living throughout our nation. Teotihuacan, already over 100 years old, was a major religious, political, and commercial center in Mexico. In China people had been using the compass, paper, seismograph, and steel for over 100 years, and portions of the Great Wall had been in existence since before the third century B.C. The apostles would have been totally overcome, had they known of these and other cultures existing far away, but still included in Christ's mandate—those "ends of the earth."

Beyond the Facts

Today Christ's followers still struggle with the magnitude of the Great Commission. Two-thirds of our world don't know Jesus as Saviour. Over 1 billion people have never even heard of Jesus, and many of them live in places where a traditional mission witness can't be given. In some countries it's a crime to become a Christian, and the punishment for disobedience is death. Most of these unreached peoples live in World A, that part of the world stretching from North Africa, through the Middle East and China, to Southeast Asia. In much of this area there are no churches, no preachers, no Bibles, and no Christians.

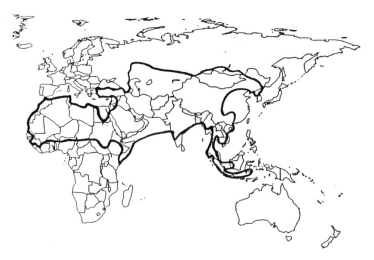

In Spite of the Facts

Because World A could never be reached with a traditional approach, new strategies emerged to allow the gospel to be known in these restricted areas of the world.

The strategy identified as of first priority, however, was not a new one at all; it was the strategy of prayer. As a result of the faithful prayers of God's people, by the end of 1992 converts had been baptized in at least 3 formerly unevangelized people groups and there were some 20 people groups where believers were gathering for the first time in modern history.

How do we, common, ordinary followers of Christ, participate in the evangelization of the world? First, we can pray daily for our missionaries and Christians throughout the world and give to the missions offerings. Knowing about the personal lives and needs of the missionaries allows us to pray more specifically for them. You can attain such information through the mission boards or in publications of Woman's Missionary Union or the Brotherhood Commission.

Perhaps God is asking you to consider going yourself to share the good news with people of another country, another culture. Whether it be for a short term or for a lifetime, following Christ to the ends of the earth brings joy indescribable and satisfaction beyond imagination.

Have you felt a particular burden for the lost people of a certain nation, city, or language? Record that people group or country in your notebook.

How did you feel when you read about the great spiritual needs of World A?

Write down three actions you can take to spread the gospel to the "ends of the earth."

[1]Richard C. Halverson, *Relevance* (Waco: Word Books, 1968), 79.

[2]Edward Schillebeeckx, *Jesus: An Experiment in Christology* (New York: Seabury Press, 1979), 156.

[3]Newsletter from the Tom Daniel family, Fall 1992.

5

Power in Weakness

Focal passage: 2 Cor. 11:21 to 12:10
Focal verse: 2 Cor. 12:9

This chapter's Bible study is from Paul's second letter to the Corinthians, chapters 11 and 12. The occasion for the writing of this second Corinthian letter is quite important if we're to understand Paul here.

Second Corinthians was written in response to a crisis in the Corinthian church. False teachers had come into Paul's Corinthian church after his departure and started to undermine everything Paul taught them and everything he stood for.

The three issues in 2 Corinthians are these: (1) the nature of the gospel, (2) the nature of true apostleship, (3) the nature of the church.

These false teachers were itinerant Jewish teachers who called themselves by the lofty name apostles. We don't know exactly who they were, but they certainly weren't any of the Twelve. They were arrogant, clever fellows, who knew how to undermine Paul's influence. They boasted of their Jewish ancestry. They boasted of their right to teach in the churches. They boasted about everything!

They seem to have valued the ecstatic gifts, such as tongues and visions, and revelations, more than anything else. They claimed they were spiritual persons. They manifested many of the characteristics associated with the term gnostic, which comes from the Greek word for knowledge, *gnosis*.

The gnostics infiltrated the church early, perhaps in the first century. By the second century they were a major problem. Though gnosticism wasn't full blown in the church until that time, biblical scholars suspect that as early as the first century the gnostics were already at work. It was the kind of quasi-religion worldview later declared to be heresy.

We must understand the attack these false teachers made on Paul. Not only did they undermine Paul's teachings, they also openly attacked and criticized Paul himself. They boasted of their own letters of recommendations from other churches.

They said, *You know, your Paul has never shown you any such letters, has he?*

They accused Paul of preaching a gospel of death. *Why, have you ever considered what this man says? He talks all the time about death, the cross, crucifixion, and suffering.* These false teachers preached a cheery gospel of life, prosperity, and success.

Furthermore, they questioned Paul's relationship to Christ. They ridiculed his weakness in speech and appearance and claimed he was inferior in knowledge. Elsewhere in the epistle Paul says, *Well, maybe I do look a little funny. Maybe I'm not the most powerful preacher that ever preached, but I'm not taking anything off of you at the point of knowledge. I'm not inferior in knowledge.* And he wasn't.

They hurled other accusations against Paul. The one that wounded him the most, I think, was that he walked *kata sarx,* according to the flesh (2 Cor. 5:16). Throughout this epistle Paul comes back to that. This charge stung him. They boasted of their own spiritual experiences and they questioned Paul's. They lived off the contributions of the church, while Paul refused any compensation from this church.

Finally, they asked, *If your Paul is such a blessed apostle of our Lord Jesus Christ, why does he have to suffer so much? Why does he have to endure such hardships, so much pain?* Which raises the question, What is the nature of true apostleship (one of the three big issues in this letter)?

Look next at the false gospel in Corinth. The gospel they preached was one of health, success, prosperity, wealth, and power.[1] This wasn't the kind of power we're talking about in this section, but a kind of self-aggrandizement. It denied the place of suffering, sacrifice, weaknesses, and brokenness in the Christian life.

This false gospel centered not on Christ's sufferings, not on the theology of the cross, but rather on these teachers themselves. It was a theology of glory.[2] In other words, they preached a self-centered worship. It went over well in Corinth; and we might suggest that it still goes over well today.

No wonder Paul was upset. Now, look at Paul's response to this alien gospel. Paul is at his best in this epistle when he is on the attack, defending himself, and engaging in polemics against his enemy. He uses irony and sarcasm to do it. He says these teachers are preaching another Jesus, a different spirit, and a different gospel (2 Cor. 11:4). That's pretty sharp.

Paul calls these intruders in his church by some choice terms. He calls them "peddlers of the word of God" (2 Cor. 2:17), "false apostles," and "super-apostles," superlative apostles (2 Cor. 11:5). They are people in love with themselves.

To their gospel of glory, Paul counters with a gospel of the cross. Jurgen Moltmann, one of the greatest twentieth-century theologians, says the cross "gives Narcissus the power to love someone else."[3]

That's what these teachers at Corinth needed. The gospel of the cross enables us to love somebody besides ourselves. So to their successful and prosperous life-style as apostles, Paul counters with a suffering discipleship. Paul knew what it was to be wounded.

Henri Nouwen speaks of those who minister as "wounded healers."[4] Are you wounded? Well then, you're ready. Are you hurting? You're ready to serve. Someone has said, "Everyone's hurting or getting ready to hurt." Do you have scars? Are you offering a good stewardship of your sufferings?

Against the idea of the church as a superchurch of successful people, Paul offered the model of servanthood. There is a lot of difference between the super church and the servant church. In the servant church the pastor is a servant, rather than a CEO, and he encourages his people to be servants.

Paul seeks to contradict the boasting of these false teachers about their superior spirituality, victorious ministries, and divine power. In 2 Corinthians the terms *boast* and *boasting* loom large. In fact, these terms occur 26 times in 2 Corinthians, and 15 of those are in chapters 11 and 12. In 2 Corinthians 11: 21-30, Paul says, *Alright, boasting is the only thing that you listen to, and since it's the only thing that impresses you, then I'm going to boast a little bit.*

"What anyone else dares to boast about—I am speaking as a fool—I also dare to boast about" (2 Cor. 11:21). I know I'm speaking as a fool, Paul confesses, and between the lines we can say, "Yes, but a fool for Christ's sake." He's foolish like a fox, this Paul.

I'm speaking like a fool. I also dare to boast of that. You've listened to these other fellows and their boasting, alright then listen to mine. Even though I know it has no profit, I'm going to do it because it's all you seem to be able to hear.

Paul is parodying the boasting of the super-apostles. We can call this passage, "Anything you can do I can do better,"[5] or the great "boast-off."

Paul isn't really trying to match these peddlers of the word of God. He is mocking them and their exalted claims. He adopts their method, which is boasting, but not their content.

What does Paul boast about? All the wrong things—imprisonments, beatings, weaknesses, hardships, and rejection. This passage drips with irony and sarcasm. In verse 30 he wraps it all up, even as he introduces the two verses that follow by saying, "If I must boast [*and apparently that is all you'll hear*], I will boast of the things that show my weakness."

In the three verses that follow, verses 31-33, Paul says, "The God and Father of the Lord Jesus, who is to be praised forever, knows that I am not lying." (v. 31). Then he goes ahead to tell them about a humiliating experience he had in the past.

Paul recounts his escape from Damascus in a basket let down over the wall. If there is any way to lose your dignity, I suppose that is it. He had to retreat from town in a hurry and no angel conducted him out of the city safely, as happened for Peter when he was conducted out of prison (Acts 12:6-11).

He wasn't able to walk through the crowd of his enemies, as Jesus did in Nazareth. For Paul there was no dramatic, dignified escape at all. Can't you just see him being lowered down in the basket? Can't you hear his critics at Corinth saying, *Have you ever heard the story about how Paul got out of Damascus? Let us tell you what happened to him.*

Paul says, *Well, I'm not going to lie about it. I'm going to boast about it. Because it shows my humiliation. It shows my weakness. It shows my complete dependence on the Lord.*

In the opening verses of chapter 12, Paul talks about visions and revelations. He says, *You guys like visions and revelations. Well, let me tell you about mine. You like to hear about unusual things. I've had more visions and revelations than all the rest of you.*

First, he told about this vision and revelation because the Corinthians liked to hear stories of visions. They'd heard them from these false teachers, so Paul tells one (2 Cor. 12:1).

Second, he described it in the third person. Something subtle is at work here. He doesn't use first person singular. He uses third person and describes something that sounds almost like somebody else's experience. He is calling attention away from himself (2 Cor. 12:2-4).

Finally, what he tells in verses 1-6 is sketchy. It tantalizes the imagination of any serious Bible student. We wish we knew more about this vision and revelation, but that is not Paul's point. He is after bigger game, and in verse 7 he begins to tell what that is.

"To keep me from being conceited because of these surpassingly great revelations, there was given me a thorn in my flesh, a messenger of Satan, to torment me" (2 Cor. 12:7).

There's been much speculation about what the thorn was, but whatever it was it obviously made Paul an object of ridicule, an easy target. Some have speculated it was epilepsy, or some kind of eye disease, or malaria. It embarrassed him terribly and his critics kept pointing to it and saying, *Well, look at this weak man. He's got this problem. We've got to feel sorry for him. It's not his fault, I suppose, but how could such a one really be an apostle? Do you think God is really blessing someone who has a problem like this?*

Since Paul regarded this thorn, at this point, as a messenger from Satan, he sought to have it removed (2 Cor. 12:8). How do you get rid of something like that? By prayer, of course.

He goes on to say, "Three times I pleaded with the Lord to take it away from me." Paul asked the Lord to remove this thorn, and every time the same answer came back. So he prayed again because he didn't get the answer he wanted.

Do you ever pray like that? "Oh, Lord, that's not what I was looking for. Let's pray about it again, Lord. Now, you see this is how it is." Three times he tried and three times the answer came back the same: "'My grace is sufficient for you, for my power is made perfect in weakness'" (2 Cor. 12:9).

If hope rises out of hopelessness, could it be that power rises out of weakness, and if so, what kind of paradox is this?

Paul, my grace is sufficient. What had originally been taken by Paul to be an obstacle to his pride, a messenger from Satan, he came to understand as a vehicle of God's grace. What if our thorns aren't so much messengers from Satan as they are occasions for the power of God?

Paul says, *When I started to see things in this new light, when I started listening to the answer that kept coming back to my prayers, my grace is sufficient, then I quit praying for this thorn to be removed any longer. I decided that if God's grace is sufficient, I could live with the thorn.*

Paul boasts of his weakness because he now sees that it embodies all the folly and weakness of the cross of Christ. In precisely this kind of weakness, the power of God is revealed. God's grace is adequate.

Karl Barth, the great Reformed theologian, perhaps the greatest theologian of the twentieth century, said, "Grace is the incomprehensible fact that God is well pleased with a man."[6]

Dietrich Bonhoeffer, a prisoner of the Nazis in 1944, was about to die. He was a dynamic young German Lutheran pastor. Some letters to a friend were smuggled out of his prison cell. In one letter, Bonhoeffer writes, "God allows Himself to be edged out of the world and on to the cross. God is weak and powerless in the world, and that is exactly the way, the only way, in which He can be with us and help us."[7]

When I am weak, then I am strong—a paradox. The Bible is full of them. The paradox of power is weakness. It sounds like foolishness to the world, but it is God's message to His people in all times.

This paradox has come in many different ways. Through the prophets that message came like this: "'Not by might nor by power, but by My Spirit,' says the Lord Almighty."

Through Jesus to the disciples, it came like this: *Apart from me you can do nothing.*

It comes to us through Paul and his second letter to the Corinthians: "'My grace is sufficient for you, for my power is made perfect in weakness'" (2 Cor. 12:9).

We are empowered by the power of God. "Ah, Sovereign Lord, . . . Nothing is too hard for you" (Jer. 32:17).

We are empowered by the power of Christ. "Who is this? Even the wind and the waves obey Him!" (Mark 4:41).

We are empowered by the Holy Spirit through prayer, for we do not know how to pray as we ought, but the Spirit intercedes for us (Rom. 8:26-27).

We are empowered to witness. "'But you will receive the power when the Holy Spirit comes on you, and you will be my witnesses'" (Acts 1:8); therefore, "why do you stand here looking into the sky?" (Acts 1:11.)

We are empowered in weakness because God's grace is sufficient and His power is made perfect in weakness (2 Cor. 12:9).

Power in Weakness

Acknowledging weakness is difficult. Although many great people have come from humble beginnings, most folks prefer to focus on elements of what is thought to be the good life—success, wealth, position, influence. Discussions centering around failures, disappointments, and shortcomings are rare. They seem only to underscore our own inabilities and foibles, and goodness knows we cannot let others see us as weak!

You would think that it would be different at church, that Christian fellowship would encourage us to be ourselves before each other—vulnerable, human, and, yes, weak. Too often, however, we feel we must hide our fears, our anxieties, our hurts, lest we be considered spiritually weak.

Just the Facts

The church should be the place where we take off our masks and confess our weaknesses. Instead, we put on a smile and a fabricated air of confidence, along with our Sunday clothes, to make ourselves presentable to the body. We find it impossible to let others see our hurt, feel our anxiety, know our anger.

Someone has said that the church is a hospital for sinners, not a haven for saints. Why, then, do we find it so difficult to acknowledge our infirmities, our weaknesses?

Beyond the Facts

Ken Medema dedicated a song to Seventh and James Baptist Church in Waco reflecting the cry of many for the true Church. It said in part:

If this is not a place where tears are understood,
Where can I go to cry?
And if this is not a place where my spirit can take wing,
Where can I go to fly?

Not only did Paul acknowledge his weaknesses, he boasted in them. Why? Because through his weakness, God's power could be revealed. "'My grace is sufficient for you, for my power is made perfect in weakness.'"

Pat Ritchie Liles was a valued staff member of the Woman's Missionary Union national office for many years. Then her life was threatened by a massive stroke. For days her life literally hung in the balance. When she miraculously survived, she immediately began physical therapy. She was told she would never walk again, but today Pat not only walks with the help of a brace, she drives herself. Although her left side remains paralyzed by the stroke and her short-term memory has been affected, Pat continues to amaze her friends with her positive outlook and strong determination.

Pat has said, "Sometimes it didn't seem worth going on,

but the Lord would put someone in front of me to say, 'Yes, it is. Keep trying. His grace is sufficient.'"

In Spite of the Facts

Much boasting we do today is misplaced. If we value those things which help us reach spiritual goals, if we truly want God's purpose for our lives, then things which bring momentary pleasure and personal ease aren't worth bragging about.

What do you boast of? Write down your honest answers.

Power in weakness is a paradox. Have you experienced such a paradox in your life? What did you learn from it?

In your quiet time today thank God for the failures, disappointments, and weaknesses which have caused you to rely more completely on Him. Ask Him to reveal to you opportunities for extending yourself to others, for capitalizing on His strength instead of your own perceived weaknesses. Remember, God's grace is sufficient.

Write down the opportunities revealed to you, and your plans to act on them.

----

[1]H. Stephen Shoemaker, *Strength in Weakness* (Nashville: Broadman Press, 1989), 19, 33.

[2]Ibid., 32.

[3]Jurgen Moltmann, *The Crucified God* (New York: Harper and Row, 1974), 72.

[4]Shoemaker, *Strength in Weakness,* 31.

[5]Ibid., 143.

[6]Karl Barth, *The Epistle to the Romans,* trans. Edwyn C. Hoskyns (London: Oxford University Press, 1965), 31.

[7]Dietrich Bonhoeffer, *Letters and Papers from Prison,* ed. Eberhard Bethge (New York: Macmillan Co., 1953), 219-20.

Section 2

Calling and Accountability

6

Called and Accountable

Focal passage: John 15:12-17
Focal verse: John 15:16

The focal passage is a succinct, compact paragraph with particular attention given to verse 16. The context is love. "'My command is this: Love each other as I have loved you'" (John 15:12).

To love people because they are human beings is noble. Humanism makes its appeal on that basis—love people, because they are like you, human beings worthy of respect and love. That's not wrong, but I know something better.

To love people because God loves them is better because it adds fullness and a Christian dimension to love. But I know something even better than that.

Jesus commands us to love one another the same way He has loved us. Here is the full-blown ethic of Jesus: "'My command is this: Love each other as I have loved you.'" So love brackets this entire paragraph. In verse 17, John returns to this theme as he closes out the paragraph. *This I command you, to love one another.* Thereby he suggests inclusion, from the very start to the end of this paragraph.

So the question for this chapter is What does it mean to be bracketed by God's love in all our existence?

John talks about the cost of this love (John 15:13). "Greater love has no man than this, that he lay down his life for his friends." The cost of love is sacrifice. *Sacrifice* is a word we seldom hear anymore, even in church. We don't even talk any longer about sacrificial giving. Let's never forget that love is a costly thing.

In verses 14 and 15, the Lord moves on to talk about servants and friends. "'I no longer call you servants, because a servant does not know his master's business. Instead, I have called you friends, for everything that I heard from my Father I have made known to you.'"

Friends of God—no elitism is involved here, as though some are servants and some are friends. Long after we become friends of God we are still servants of God. The point seems to be that friends know what the family is doing. Because Christ has made known to us the mind of God and the intentions of God, we are the friends of God. We know what He is about.

You Did Not Choose Me

This brings up verse 16—the focal verse for this chapter and several chapters to come. "'You did not choose me.'" None of us left to ourselves ever chooses God. This verse is a statement of our sin, and sin is always a mystery. Paul calls it "the mystery of our iniquity" (2 Thess 2:7 KJV). Sin is a mystery—inexplicable, irrational, and consists of this: We haven't chosen God. We haven't called on God.

Paul expressed it like this. "For I have the desire to do what is good, but I cannot carry it out. For what I do is not the good I want to do; no, the evil I do not want to do—this I keep on doing" (Rom. 7:18-19).

Psychologist and therapist John Bradshaw has spoken of this as the language of addiction. Sin is an addiction, irrational and inexplicable. Bradshaw talks about "the hole in our souls."[1] What a graphic description of sin!

"You did not choose me"—that is, you did not call on me. Between the lines we have to read, *"You could have, but you didn't."*

Jesus said, "This is the verdict: Light has come into the world, but men loved darkness instead of light because their deeds were evil" (John 3:19). The Bible is the book that traces our choices, our divided mind.

But even this isn't the full extent of our choices. We didn't choose God, and that in itself was bad enough. But in addition to that we chose to replace God with other things.

The universal presupposition of the gospel is this: *We have not chosen God.* This is the point where grace begins.

But I Did Choose (Call) You

"But I chose you." *I did call you. You have not called on me, but I have called on you.* This is what theologians call *election.* It means choice, selection, being called. Abraham was called. Israel was called. Believers are called. In Romans 8:30 Paul speaks of God's elect, those who are called.

In choosing, in electing, and in calling, God always takes the initiative. God makes the first move. Ours is a seeking God whom we seek only because He has already found us.

Remember the lyrics from the old song "Victory in Jesus"? "He loved me ere I knew Him." This is what the biblical scholars call prevenient grace, common grace, general revelation, the sunshine and the rain that fall on the just and the unjust.

God so wants us to know Him that He spares no medium in making Himself known. God speaks in many voices instead of one; He sings in chorus rather than solo. God strains language, poetry, art, music, and word in order to get through to us. The reason for God's choice of us is to be found only in His grace.

August Lecerf says, "The key to the Old Testament is the word nevertheless."[2] In Psalm 89 we read, "I will punish their sin with the rod, their iniquity with flogging; but I will not take my love from him" (Psalm 89:32-33).

Grace is God's "nevertheless" which He writes across our failure. We wax eloquent in preaching and teaching grace, but what we really practice is works, isn't it? We seem to live as though we get one good dose of grace when we're converted, but from then on it's everybody for himself.

I want to tell you, it's grace all the way. It's grace every day.

You are chosen for service, not for favoritism. God's people are chosen to be humanity's exposed nerve, not for privilege, but for service. Jesus was God's chosen one. But that choice led Him to a cross rather than to the throne in Rome. The nearest we ever come in the scripture to having a reason for God's love and God's call is His love. The context is love. It brackets this paragraph. It brackets our lives.

We must admit up front that Matthew 22:14 (KJV) is a difficult verse. "For many are called, but few are chosen." Only Matthew seems to make a great deal out of this.

In the fifth century, Augustine made the classic formulation of the doctrine of election. In the sixteenth century the Protestant reformer, John Calvin, came along and revised Augustine's work, emphasizing the sovereignty of God almost to the point of denying free will.

After Calvin's death his disciples took up the argument. One of them, Theodore Beza, hardened this doctrine of election, or predestination, into what is now known as double predestination. He taught that some are called to salvation, and some are called to condemnation.[3] I would suggest that nothing could be further from the spirit of Christ than that.

Donald Baillie, in his profound book *God Was in Christ*, speaks of the paradox of grace, and he says the paradox of grace is that we know surely that we did choose to follow Christ, but somehow we know that before we chose to follow Him, He chose us.[4] As we enter the door of God's opportunity, the door of grace, on the outside we seem to read, *Whosoever will may come.* Having stepped through the door and looked back, we discover that over the door on the inside there are the words, "You did not choose me, but I chose you."

Somebody has said that the elect are the whosoever wills and the nonelect are the whosoever won'ts. *I chose you and did not reject others.*

Appointed to Bear Fruit

"I have appointed you to bear fruit." If called means chosen or elected, then accountable means stewardship. "So then, each of us will give an account of himself to God" (Rom.

14:12). Bear fruit. That's our mission, our accountability.

Galatians 5:22-23 lists some of the fruits of the spirit: Love, joy, peace, patience, kindness, goodness, faithfulness, gentleness, and self-control. Before we can bear any fruit in the sense of missions accomplished, we must first cultivate the fruit of the spirit.

Now this fruit isn't just any old fruit, but fruit that abides, that remains. The word that John uses here for fruit that abides is *menein*, one of John's favorite and most complex terms. He uses this term 40 times, and in 7 different ways. The three synoptic Gospels—Matthew, Mark, and Luke—use this term collectively only about a dozen times.

John loves this term, and though he has seven different meanings for it, two meanings are primary. To remain in something or on something is the first one; and to be intimately united with someone is the second. It's a stronger form of Paul's great term *in Christ*.[5] *Menein* is translated various ways—"remain," "abide," "stay," "dwell"; but John 15 refers to the permanence of the fruit. Since we are called, we are also accountable to bear fruit that abides.

John concluded verse 16 by talking about asking the Father in Jesus' name. "'Then the Father will give you whatever you ask in my name.'" He now mentions prayer. Isn't that interesting? Already in this paragraph He has mentioned our sin: "You did not choose me"; He has mentioned our calling: "but I chose you"; and He has mentioned our accountability: "and appointed you to go and bear fruit." Now He talks about prayer.

Remember that God has the first word. Just as God makes the first move, God also has the first word. In creation that word was *Let there be*. In covenant that word was, *I shall be your God and you shall be my people*. The first word was God's in incarnation because in the fullness of time Christ came. In salvation God has the first word, *You have not chosen me, but I have chosen you. You did not call on me, even though you could have; but I have called on you*. There is no debate about giving God the first word.

What then is prayer?

Prayer is answering speech.[6] We do not initiate anything;

we only respond. Blaise Pascal, the great French Christian philosopher, said, "I would not now be seeking thee, if I had not already been found of thee."[7]

Where does John end this paragraph? The same place he began. Love one another. The end is the same as the beginning. What does it mean, then, that our sin, our calling, our accountability, our missions, and our prayer are all bracketed by love? It means, I think, that the love of God is adequate for whatever we bring to it.

When we think about the great callings in the Bible, what do we usually think of? Moses at the burning bush; Samuel, the boy called in the night; Jeremiah, the man who said he was too young to be a prophet; Isaiah with the vision of God transcendent high and lifted up; and Saul of Tarsus, turned around in his tracks, blinded by a light from heaven, knocked to his knees—these are some of the Bible's great callings.

But I have decided not to examine any of those callings for three reasons: First, they are all male; second, they are all well known; and third, these people were called in isolated circumstances and lived lonely lives, in many cases serving by themselves.

Let's speak about another group: Abraham and Sarah; Mary and Joseph; Jesus' disciples; and finally the Easter people of John 20, particularly Mary Magdalene. Why speak about these callings? They involve men and women; they are callings less familiar to us as callings; and they were called in pairs or groups to serve in mutuality and community.

The question for the next chapter is this: What happens when one person's calling hooks another person's accountability? And we'll put names on that situation: Abraham and Sarah.

Called and Accountable

When it seemed that all humanity might be eternally lost in the wilderness of sin, the Father sent His very Son to tell us He loved us and wanted to find us, save us. Scarcely had we recovered from the sense of awe at being chosen, when God said to us, *Now, you go and let someone else know of my offer of love and salvation.*

To just anyone, Lord?
To everyone. Whosoever will may come.

Just the Facts

Everyone enjoys being called. Do you remember those childhood days of choosing up sides for games? Do you remember how carefully you listened for one of the team captains to call your name? Occasionally, the captain was a special friend and called your name first, not because you were particularly good at the game, but just because she liked you.

God's call isn't related to our worthiness to be chosen, nor does He play favorites. He calls us because of who He is, not who we are. His call is personal, irrevocable, and undeserved.

While we could never merit His salvation, to receive it places certain demands upon us. Jesus urges His followers to share His invitation to eternal life with others.

"We love because he first loved us" (1 John 4:19). There are those all around us who would love Him, too, if they only knew of His desire to receive them.

A billboard advertising a large variety store chain claimed, "To find us is to love us." Christ would say, however, *To love them, is to find them.* His love compels us to seek the lost.

Beyond the Facts

To reduce the meaning of missions to its essence, would result in the following:

God loves me.
God loves everyone in the world.
Not everyone knows that.
He wants me to go and tell.

Yet most of us, like Moses, can think of numerous reasons not to obey His call. Read this story again in Exodus 3 and 4 and be reminded of how Moses' excuses are like yours. Finally, Moses blurted out, *Let someone else do it.* God's response to his outburst is sobering: "Then the Lord's anger burned against Moses" (Ex. 4:13). What heart committed to the Father could bear this indictment!

God's call requires a response. Samuel, as a little boy in the tabernacle, responded: "'Speak, for your servant is listening'" (1 Sam. 3:10). Isaiah replied: "'Here am I. Send me!'" (Isa. 6:8). The one who calls always expects an answer.

In Spite of the Facts

God calls not only the Isaiahs and the Samuels. He calls ordinary people too—people like you and me. He calls us first to repentance and new life. Billy Graham has said, "Conversion is so simple that the smallest child can be converted, but it is also so profound that theologians throughout history have pondered the depth of its meaning."[8]

Have you accepted God's call to come to Him? If not, there is no better time to say, "'Speak, Lord, for your servant is listening.'" Saying yes to God's call will bring joy, peace, and forgiveness in your life. What a thought!

While God calls us to come, He also calls us to mature, to bear fruit which endures. Galatians 5:22-23 lists fruits of the Spirit. Consider them.

Love	Patience	Faithfulness
Joy	Kindness	Gentleness
Peace	Goodness	Self-control

These are the enduring fruits of the Spirit. Which one needs the most attention in your own spiritual development? Is it patience? Self-control? Select one and begin to pray that the Spirit will lead you in moving toward maturity in that area. Use a concordance to find Scripture verses which deal with that area. Pray for sensitivity to the need for growth during every moment of your day. "So I say, live by the Spirit, and you will not gratify the desires of the sinful nature" (Gal. 5:16).

Write down the fruit you have focused on. Also write down the accompanying Scripture verses. Memorize the verses.

Finally, God calls us to be on mission for Him. All of life is an opportunity to serve Him. What is He asking you to do?

Will you say yes? "You are a Christian today because some-body cared. Now, it's your turn."[9]

Think of one person who is not a Christian with whom you come in contact on a regular basis. Claim that person for Christ, and pray daily for his or her salvation. Ask God to give you the courage and opportunities to share your own experience and commitment to Christ. You could well be the only Christian who touches that person's life. You are called and accountable.

Write down the person's name and your pledge to pray and share. Date your entry.

---

[1]John Bradshaw, *The Family* (Deerfield Beach, FL: Health Communications, Inc., 1988), 5.

[2]J. S. Whale, *Victor and Victim* (Cambridge: University Press, 1960), 10.

[3]T. H. L. Parker, "Predestination," in *A Dictionary of Christian Theology* (Philadelphia: Westminster Press, 1969), 264-69.

[4]D. M. Baillie, *God Was in Christ* (New York: Charles Scribner's Sons, 1948), 114-32.

[5]Raymond E. Brown, *The Gospel According to John (1-12)*, vol. 29 of *The Anchor Bible* (Garden City, NY: Doubleday and Co.), 510-11.

[6]Eugene H. Peterson, *Working the Angles: The Shape of Pastoral Integrity* (Grand Rapids: Wm. B. Eerdmans Pub. Co., 1987), 32.

[7]Hugh Thomson Ken, Jr., "The Song of Songs, Text, Exegesis, and Exposition," in *The Interpreter's Bible,* ed. George Arthur Buttrick (Nashville: Abingdon Press, 1956), vol. 5, 112.

[8]Billy Graham, *Quotations for the Christian World,* ed. Edythe Draper (Wheaton, IL: Tyndale House Publisher Inc., 1992), 106.

[9]Albert M. Wells, Jr., ed. *Inspiring Quotations* (Nashville: Thomas Nelson, 1988), 36.

7

Abraham and Sarah: Called to Venture, Accountable to Obey

Focal passages: Genesis 12:1-5; 17:15-19; Romans 4:18-22; Hebrews 11:8-12
Focal verses: Genesis 12:1; 17:15-16; Romans 4:20-21; Hebrews 11:8

The Bible has two literal meanings of the terms *call* and *calling*. These meanings shape the uses of these terms everywhere. The first one is "to give a name," to call someone by name. Knowledge begins with the naming of a thing, as, for instance, when we read in Genesis, "God called the light 'day.'"

The second biblical meaning of the terms *call* or *calling* is "to summon." That is to demand an appearance, to demand that someone come into your presence.[1] Matthew writes that Herod secretly summoned the wise men.

In the calling of Abraham we see the beginning of the biblical process of election, or calling and accountability. Abraham's call is the moment when a people are born, when a hope is first nurtured. Abraham is mentioned some 70 times in the New Testament and almost always in connection with faith. He is the Bible's grand old man of faith.

Three magnificent chapters deal with the faith of Abraham. The first one is Genesis 12 and following; the second is Romans 4; and the third is Hebrews 11. All three chapters tell something unique about the faith of Abraham and Sarah.

Let Go

Abraham and Sarah were called and accountable to let go, to release. "The Lord had said to Abraham, 'Leave your country, your people and your father's household and go to the land I will show you'" (Gen. 12:1).

Abraham was called to leave the past behind and to set out on a great adventure to a new land. His calling meant letting go of some things that must have been precious to him. He was asked to let go of his country, his kindred, his family, his father's household. His father would live another 60 years and Abraham would never see him again.

One thing Abraham did not let go—his wife, Sarah. Abraham received the call of God, but from the start Sarah was implicated. She had to let go too—of family, kindred, home, father, security, and comfort. Abraham's call made Sarah accountable. We haven't always noted that, have we?

Faith as letting go may be a new idea to us because we have been taught that faith is what we can hold on to against the ravages of time and the worms of doubt. But for the sake of his calling and the possibility of a new dimension of faith, Abraham became accountable for letting go of some things.

How prepared are we to change, to give up, to release? Sometimes things die. Sometimes they refuse to change, which is just as bad.

Tennyson poses the question for us: "For who would keep an ancient form through which the spirit breathes no more?"[2] All our life long we do let go. We let go of childhood and youthful dreams. Gradually we let go of the prime of our lives. Then we let go of health and strength. Finally we let go of life itself.

Life wants to teach us how to let go. Why must we always construe faith as somehow totally different from life? Faith is surrender. Faith is release. We never do make an easy peace with this paradox in our faith that we actually win by losing, live by dying, keep by giving away, and hold fast only by letting go.

In Hebrew to have faith means to make one's self secure in God. Abraham's calling and consequent accountability were directed toward God's plans for the future. Somebody has said that faith is a risk supported by a memory and a promise. For Abraham there was the memory of God's calling in the past. But out ahead of him was a promise, and he believed that promise. He had made himself secure in God.

Ignazio Silone, in that marvelous novel, *Bread and Wine,* says, "We must not become obsessed with the idea of security. . . . Spiritual life does not go with a secure life. You have to take risks."[3] We know about the certainties and securities of faith, but do we know about the risks in faith?

Abraham and Sarah were called and accountable to let go of some things. Why? Because God had other things to give them and as long as their hands were full, they couldn't accept these new things.

Trust God's Promise

Paul writes, concerning Abraham: "Yet he did not waver through unbelief regarding the promise of God, but was strengthened in his faith and gave glory to God, being fully persuaded that God had power to do what he had promised" (Rom. 4:20).

These promises concerned three things: righteousness, children, and the inheritance of all the earth. One might argue that there was every reason for Abraham and Sarah not to trust God's promises. God kept promising these things in the distant future. Abraham was asked to believe against all probabilities, or as Paul expresses it, in hope against hope (Rom. 4:18).

Karl Barth described Abraham's faith: "This is Abraham's faith: faith which, in hope against hope, steps out beyond human capacity across the chasm which separates God and man. . . . We watch Abraham as he advances to the place where he is supported only by the word of God."[4] That's faith.

God kept making seemingly impossible promises to Abraham and to Sarah. The only thing that stands between us and eternity is the promise. But whose promise is it? We never escape the promissory nature of faith.

God is always out there in the future for us, ahead of us. Prepositions are so important in the way we place our God. Sometimes we say God is with us, or above us, or within us, or behind us, or around us. But never forget that God is ahead of us, out there in the future.

Abraham would have answered the question Where is your God? by saying, *He's out there. He's out there in the future. And He has called me from that future and said, "Abraham, come on out here and meet me. There's nothing you need fear."*

From the start Sarah was implicated in all of this—the promise and the call. In Hebrews 11:11 a special New Testament tribute is given her. "By faith, Abraham, even though he was past age—and Sarah herself was barren—was enabled to become a father because he considered him faithful who had made the promise."

There's the key. He was faithful Who had promised.

Her involvement in this calling and accountability was that first her name was changed. She had always been Sarai. Now her name was changed to Sarah, which meant "princess." Her name actually meant the same thing as it had before. But while previously she had been called princess, now she was to become one and she was to act like one. Furthermore, she would be blessed by the gift of a son. Sarah would thus become a mother of nations.

God's greatest promises to us always involve a child. Abraham and Sarah were learning how to live by the promises. At this latter promise that Sarah would become a mother in her old age and Abraham a father, Abraham fell on his face, convulsed with laughter. (Well, I guess so. He was 100 years old.)

In Genesis 18 Sarah had a good laugh outside the tent door at the promise of the Lord that she would become a mother (Gen. 18:12). Sarah was almost 90.

God took offense. He said, "'Why did Sarah laugh and say,

"Will I really have a child, now that I am old?" Is anything too hard for the Lord?' " (Gen. 18:13-14).

It wasn't reasonable, certainly not probable, that Sarah and Abraham would become parents at their age. It wasn't congruent. It wasn't even possible. Was it? For this old couple to have a child?

And so, they laughed. Can't you hear them? The bitter, scornful laugh, the laugh of skepticism, the laugh of holy hilarity. But just a few months later, when their son was born, the laughing stopped. Or perhaps it just began, because they named him Isaac, which means "laughter." So, aged Abraham and Sarah bought diapers, and invested in a rocking chair, and built a little crib with a swinging mobile on it. They fixed up a nursery, and spent sleepless nights up with their baby, Laughter. And they stood long, silent periods by the crib with their old wrinkled hands clasping one another because God's promise had finally come to pass with Sarah's child.

Called to Obey

Abraham and Sarah were called to obey, even without knowing everything.

For that insight we look at Hebrews 11, one of the great chapters in the New Testament. "By faith Abraham, when called to go to a place he would later receive as his inheritance; obeyed and went, even though he did not know where he was going. By faith he made his home in the promised land like a stranger in a foreign country; he lived in tents, as did Isaac and Jacob, who were heirs with him of the same promise. For he was looking forward to the city with foundations, whose architect and builder is God" (Heb. 11:8-10).

He went out not knowing. He didn't know where he was to go, why he had been called, or how God would fulfill His promises. Doesn't that suggest that maybe faith has nothing to do with knowing where, or how, or why?

But calling and accountability have everything to do with obedience. Faith makes a start, even when it doesn't yet know everything.

If we must know exactly where we're going, then the chances are that we're not following. Faith is obedience.

Someone has said, "The place God calls you to is the place where your deep gladness and the world's deep hunger meet."

The writer of Hebrews says that Abraham and Sarah were foreigners even in the land of promise. Think about that. They were where God wanted them to be. They were in the land of promise to which He had led them and they were still foreigners. They looked forward to a city, but the city wasn't there yet. They looked forward to a new city.

Those who are called and hence accountable are known as pilgrims, visionaries, foreigners, and exiles. That's us. We are the people who have seen the city in the distance and must yet camp in the desert one more night. Do God's people not like the wilderness anymore? In that wilderness we have made our best contributions because we have learned that faith is ever at its best on the edge of weakness.

Hebrews 11:11 says that for Sarah, faith was the power to conceive. Abraham was called and Sarah was implicated. What happens when your calling hooks someone else's accountability? Do you suppose it could have worked the other way? What if Sarah had been the called one? Could it have still worked? Well, it did work that way, centuries later to a couple named Mary and Joseph, and remembered forever in that order—Mary and Joseph.

Abraham and Sarah were called to venture and accountable to obey God, and so are we. It won't be easy.

Abraham and Sarah:
Called to Venture, Accountable to Obey

When Bill and I went to live as missionaries in Indonesia, we were told we could take only a limited amount of goods. Should we take the baby bed or a couch, books or photography equipment? Each decision had to be made carefully to cover needs in a land we had never seen, under living circumstances about which we knew little.

The description of Abraham's departure from Ur of the Chaldeans to an unknown destination was quite different. Abraham and Sarah took all their household goods, servants, and animals. (You can take a lot more when it doesn't have to fit on a ship!) In a day when most people were born, lived, and died in the same location, Abraham and Sarah left their families to go to an unknown place. Why? Because they were called—called to venture.

Just the Facts

Sometimes staying in the same place is a greater risk than being willing to move. Consider the businessman given a promotion by his corporation if he moves to another city. To advance his career, he must be willing to relocate. However, his family has joined a church where every member of the family is maturing spiritually and is joyfully involved. Can he risk declining advancement in order to ensure his family's spiritual needs?

Beyond the Facts

Being willing to venture, to risk, in response to God's call may be less related to geography today than it was in Abraham's time. To go or to stay—either option may require the highest commitment.

William Carey, 200 years ago, left his home in England to go to faraway India to take the gospel to the millions who hadn't heard. Today, some 4,000 Southern Baptist foreign missionaries serve in distant places, sometimes leaving their adult children and their parents at home.

Sometimes we too are asked to let go of material things to follow Christ's call. When asked by new missionaries if they should take certain belongings to the foreign field, Baker James Cauthen would always respond: "Take whatever you like, but take them in your hands, not in your heart." That is good advice whether you stay or go. Hold things lightly in your hands. They can never bring the joy that embracing Christ bestows.

Christ also asks us sometimes to let go of people. It is often tempting to tie those we love closely to us, preventing their freedom to follow God's will for their lives. Letting go of our loved ones may be the greatest sacrifice we can ever make.

In Spite of the Facts

When given the opportunity to go snorkeling, I had mixed emotions. Only someone who's been snorkeling and has forgotten to breathe through the mouth can know the terror of coming up choking on salt water. Overcoming the natural habit of breathing through the nose in order to use the snorkeling gear is somewhat difficult, but once mastered it allows glimpses into some of God's most beautiful creation. Reveling in the magnificence of hidden beauty makes the risk of attempting something new well worth the while.

Far greater are the spiritual wonders the Father wants to reveal to us, if we are willing to step out on faith. Too many of us lose the opportunity to experience true exhilaration of spirit, because we are fearful of risking. God would tell us to launch out into the deep. Victories come only to those willing to strive. The discoveries of life come only through venturing into the unknown.

What is Christ asking you to release? The comforts and joy of home? The treasures you hold in your hand? The presence of someone dearer than life itself?

Take a few moments to write in your journal the things Christ is asking you to release. Record your feelings about giving up those things. Ask the Spirit to make you bold, to provide you with the faith of Abraham and Sarah. Take the first step in following Him. That's the hardest one.

---

[1] J. P. Thornton-Duesbery, "Call, Called, Calling," in *A Theological Word Book of the Bible,* ed. Alan Richardson (New York: Macmillan Co., 1958), 39.

[2] Alfred Lord Tennyson, "In Memoriam," in *Victorian and Later English Poets* (New York: American Book Co., 1949), 79.

[3] Ignazio Silone, *Bread and Wine* (New York: New American Library, 1962), 265.

[4] Karl Barth, *The Epistle to the Romans,* trans. Edwyn C. Hoskyns (London: Oxford University Press, 1965), 142.

8

Mary and Joseph: Called to Wonder, Accountable to Be Faithful

Focal passages: Luke 1:26-38; Matthew 1:18-21
Focal verse: Luke 1:37

In Luke 1 and Matthew 1, first Mary, and then Joseph, learn from an angel what is about to occur in God's plan and in their lives.

Striking parallels exist between the Mary and Joseph story in the New Testament and the Abraham and Sarah story in the Old Testament. Both couples received a birth announcement from God.

In both cases the calling from God was wrapped up in the promise of a child. For Abraham and Sarah, it was too late to have a baby. For Mary and Joseph, it was too early. Both were called to have unusual faith and in both instances disbelief and incredulity attended the birth announcement. Abraham and Sarah responded by laughing. Mary responded by asking a question: "'How will this be?'" For both couples, there was the waiting period when doubt gradually melted away into faith and wonder at God's ways. With both couples the calling from God came first to one of the pair, to Abraham and to Mary, while the spouse was necessarily implicated.

And so we come back to the question, what happens when your calling hooks my accountability? What's to be said about the Sarahs and Josephs, who just happen to be in the right place at the right time?

Response to a Calling: Mary

The angels were busy about this time, according to Luke and Matthew. Gabriel was dispatched to Zechariah to inform him that he would become the father of the forerunner of Messiah. Just a little while after that, once again, Gabriel was dispatched, this time to bring a message to the maid Mary, who was busy at home. He brought her the message that she would become the mother of Messiah. Later an angel (we're not told if it was Gabriel) appeared to Joseph in a dream.

Gabriel appeared to Zechariah in the Temple in Jerusalem. The Temple is where we might expect a visit from God. But with Mary, something new occurs. God now speaks to Mary outside the Temple.[1]

Where else could God have spoken to Mary? As a woman, she was forbidden from certain temple precincts. If God wanted a word with Mary He had to meet her outside the temple.

We need to take our visits from God where we find them. If God makes visits outside the holy place then let's be alert to them, welcome them, be ready for them. If we can't find God in the secular everyday world, we may lose God altogether.

Surely God is at work in many places outside the temple. Let's look for Him and listen for Him. The world, unfortunately, no longer comes to church. But God makes house calls outside of the temple, and that's where He found Mary.

Gabriel greets Mary as "highly favored by God." No mention is made in the text of Mary's worth or her virtue. If she's been singled out by God, grace alone is responsible.

Look at Mary's response. First, it was fear (Luke 1:29-30). "Mary was greatly troubled at his words and wondered what kind of greeting this might be. But the angel said to her, 'Do not be afraid, Mary, you have found favor with God.'"

That God should concern Himself with her caused Mary great fear. It's as though verse 29 is the end of one era in history and verse 30 is the opening of a new era. The darkness of fear is coming to a close. From this point on in the New Testament, we hear again and again the injunction not to be afraid. Shepherds on the Bethlehem plains are told "Do not be afraid." Peter at the Resurrection is told "Fear not." This command puts an end to fear. Fear isn't the last word any longer.[2]

Mary's second response to her calling was perplexity (Luke 1:31-37). In response to Gabriel's announcement that she would conceive and bear a son, Mary asked, "How will this be?" (Luke 1:34). Mary is simply voicing that question for all of us who stand in the covenant tradition.

Fear has already begun to change to wonder, and the wonder has come to stay. This simple Jewish maiden has come face-to-face with the incomprehensibility of God! There is no answer to her question except God himself. There is only grace. The sheer givenness of grace has been flung down among us. If Mary were chosen, if she were called, then we don't have to look further than the grace of God for a reason.

It is a very human question that Mary asked, the question, "'How will this be?'" But *how* is never ultimately the question that concerns God nor is it the question that occupies the biblical writers.

God is concerned with an altogether different question. Do you remember that great hymn based on 2 Timothy 1:12? "I know whom I have believed, and am persuaded that He is able to keep that which I've committed unto Him." Remember the verses and the stanza of it? "I know not why God's wondrous Grace to me He hath made known. . . . I know not how (that's the question Mary asked, "'How will this be?'") this saving faith to me He did impart." At the center of the Bible there is a Whom, a person; and the question that God is most concerned with is this *who* question.

When Mary asked the *how* question, "How will this be?"

the angel answers the *who* question. "For nothing is impossible with God" (Luke 1:37). What a grand answer to a *how* question! The angel echoes God's question to Abraham and Sarah in Genesis 18 when God says, "Is anything too hard for the Lord?" (Gen. 18:14). Centuries later that question gets an answer from Gabriel. *With God nothing is impossible.*

Mary's third response to her calling is trust (Luke 1:38). God calls Mary to a life of wonder that would never quite be dispelled. She would always wonder about her Son, at the things He was doing and the things He was saying and oh! those people He associated with. Mary was always left to wonder. Her Son was always a puzzle to her. She would keep many of these things, pondering them in her heart; but at this moment when God called her, this young Jewish maiden was overwhelmed. God called Mary, and waited for her reply.

Mary's response to the angel was humble trust, "I am the Lord's servant," followed by willing obedience, "May it be to me as you have said" (Luke 1:38).

Response to a Calling: Joseph

Meanwhile, just across town, there was another problem. No angel had as yet come to Joseph. Joseph's response was somewhat different from Mary's. In Matthew 1:20, the angel came to Joseph.

At first Joseph was terribly disappointed to learn about Mary's situation. He had had such hopes for their marriage. They were now betrothed, but Jews considered a betrothal as permanent as a marriage. Now it appeared that Mary was not the woman he had thought. She was pregnant and Joseph was crushed. His world caved in, and being a just man, he felt bound by the law to divorce Mary.

There were two ways of doing divorce. He could do it in a public way, in which case Mary would be subject to stoning, under Jewish law. Or he could do it in a private way, putting her away quietly, which required only two witnesses. While he was a just man, his justice was tempered by something else. It was tempered by mercy (Matt. 1:19). He was unwilling to put her to shame, not to mention danger.

Put yourself in Mary's place. How could you explain this to

your fiancé? *Uh, Joe, honey, there's something you've got to under-stand. Before we're married, I have to have this baby, promised to me by an angel.* Would you buy that, short of a conversation with the angel yourself? Fred Craddock, great New Testament scholar and professor of preaching at Emory University, says that God's call to His messenger has seldom been loud enough for the rest of the family to hear.[3]

Joseph was disappointed at first. Joseph was also fearful, as Mary had been, but for a different reason (Matt. 1:20). For the angel said to him, *Joseph, do not be afraid that your status as a just and righteous man will be stained in any way by taking Mary as your wife because that which is conceived of her is by the Holy Spirit.*

"How will this be?" By the Holy Spirit. The central point in this passage is the role of the Holy Spirit. Joseph is now given power, along with Mary, to name their child. And His name shall be Jesus, which means "Yahweh will save."

In Matthew 1:22-23 is recorded Joseph's third response to this calling. "All this took place to fulfill what the Lord had said through the prophet: 'The virgin will be with child and will give birth to a son, and they will call him Immanuel'— which means 'God with us.'" This passage, Isaiah 7:14, is one of the most interesting passages in the prophecy of Isaiah. Immanuel is to the Gospel of Matthew what the *Word,* the *Logos,* is to the Gospel of John.

You remember the prologue to the Gospel of John, "In the beginning was the Word, and the Word was with God." Then a few verses later, "The Word became flesh and made his dwelling among us."

Immanuel serves the same purpose in Matthew's Gospel. To make sure that we understand the meaning of Immanuel, Matthew interprets it. It means, he says, "God with us." So at the beginning of the Gospel of Matthew is this Scripture verse from Isaiah which means "God with us." At the end of the Gospel of Matthew Jesus is saying good-bye to His disciples. "I am with you always."

Matthew's Gospel opens with Joseph's calling to be Mary's husband. *It's alright, Joseph, go ahead. And you will serve also as the earthly father of God's Son. It's alright, Joseph, go ahead.* At the end of Matthew's Gospel is accountability. *Go into the world and make disciples and I am with you always.*

Matthew's Gospel is bracketed by calling, response, accountability, and the assurance of God's presence with us.

Finally (Matt. 1:24), look at what Joseph's response eventually was: obedience. He did as the angel commanded him. When Mary's child was born, Joseph didn't forget his dream. He named the child Jesus as he had been instructed.

Joseph is the forgotten man of Christmas. It took courage and understanding to embrace Mary's child as his own. Here was a truly secure and trusting man. When Joseph realized that Mary's calling was from God, that she had been chosen by God to become the mother of Christ, then Joseph affirmed what God had affirmed. What else could a husband do who loves the Lord? He had to affirm what God had affirmed. Joseph then became the supportive caretaker of the mother of Christ, as well as the Son of God. (What do you suppose that attitude on Joseph's part did for their marriage in later years?)

I suppose we'll never get used to the wonders of God's ways. Much of what we know about God we have learned through our families, and those who loved us and cared for us. Mary and Joseph, called to wonder, accountable to be faithful, even while they wondered. May we never lose the wonder of our calling. This whole question of calling and accountability impinges on home, family, and marriage. Families find themselves today in fluid roles as it becomes more possible for everyone to find fulfillment.

The telephone rings, and it's God calling, and today anyone can answer.

Mary and Joseph:
Called to Wonder, Accountable to Obey

The wise men wondered at the star that suddenly, miraculously appeared in the sky, luring them from their laboratories into an eternal quest for what? Only a tiny baby? Their gifts of gold, frankincense, and myrrh gave evidence to their certainty that this was not just any baby, but King and God and Sacrifice.

The object of the shepherds' wonder was the host of angels suddenly appearing in the night, praising God and saying: "Glory to God in the highest, and on earth peace to men on whom his favor rests."

Simeon, righteous and devout, and Anna, faithful prophetess, wondered that among all the seekers and worshipers in the temple, they were permitted to see *God's salvation, the light of revelation to the Gentiles, and the redemption of Jerusalem.*

But the wonder of Mary and Joseph was the most magnificent—wonder that the tiny baby cradled in her arms fulfilled the promise of the gift of God's Son. The infant was tangible reward to the faithfulness of Mary and Joseph. Amazing! God in human form!

Just the Facts

When we read the Christmas story, it's easy for us to trivialize the trauma of the waiting period experienced by Mary and Joseph. How many times during those nine months must they have relived the angel Gabriel's announcement and whispered again, "'How will this be?'" Even though the message was delivered by God's special courier, their confidence must have waned at times. Their fear and perplexity surely returned to cause them to question God's plan.

Beyond the Facts

What caused Mary and Joseph to continue to believe that God would do what He said He would do? Faith—"being sure of what we hope for and certain of what we do not see" (Heb. 11:1). Faith is the necessary element if we come to Him. "And without faith it is impossible to please God, because anyone who comes to him must believe that he exists and that he rewards those who earnestly seek him" (Heb. 11:6).

God tested the faith of Mary and Joseph by calling for their obedience in the midst of questions and fear. Perhaps He is asking you to respond to His call with obedience, just as He did Mary and Joseph. Can you say with Mary, "May it be to me as you have said"?

In Spite of the Facts

The greatest wonder of all isn't just that God became man, born of a virgin. The most amazing thing is that He came on my behalf and yours, offering salvation and restoration through His sacrifice. The only appropriate response to His treasured gift is obedience.

C. H. Dodd has said, "To know God is to experience His love in Christ, and to return that love in obedience."[4] Jesus said, "If you love me, you will obey what I command" (John 14:15). The measure of our love for God is found in our willingness to obey. Obedience requires listening, yielding, and trust. God calls us to be willing to risk; and when we do, two miracles occur: He works in us and He works through us. Awesome thought!

Meditate now on what obedience God is calling for in your life. What risks is He calling for? Write down your thoughts.

Are you fearful of this risk? Why or why not?

How does the story of Mary and Joseph help you face your calling?

––––––
[1]Karl Barth, *The Great Promise: Luke I* (New York: Philosophical Library, 1963), 21.

[2]Ibid., 25.

[3]Fred Craddock, E. Y. Mullins Lectures on Preaching, Southern Baptist Theological Seminary, Louisville, KY, March 1987. Available on tape.

[4]Albert M. Wells, Jr., ed. *Inspiring Quotations* (Nashville: Thomas Nelson, 1988), 143.

9

Disciples: Called to Follow, Accountable to Become

Focal passage: Mark 1:16-18
Focal verse: Mark 1:17

Not once, but many times, Jesus said, "Follow me." To Peter and Andrew by the Sea of Galilee Jesus said, "Follow me . . . and I will make you fishers of men." To James and John with their father mending nets He said, "Follow me." To a reluctant disciple He said, "'Follow me, and let the dead bury their own dead." To a rich young ruler Jesus said, "Go, sell everything you have and give it to the poor. . . . Then come, follow me."

To all would-be disciples Jesus still says, "If anyone would come after me, he must deny himself and take up his cross and follow me."

What does it mean to follow Jesus? It means to present Him your life as a blank check and permit Him to fill in the amount. It is to master the fine art of fishing, to embark on a long journey, to find your story within His story, to fall in love

76

with what He is in love with. The metaphors are endless.

But most of all, to follow Jesus is to learn Who He is and what He expects.

Follow Me—I Know Where I'm Going

What is Christ saying to all would-be disciples when He calls to follow Him? He is saying, *Follow me because I know where I'm going.* Jesus had a sense of purpose that made people want to follow Him.

In the Gospel of Luke Jesus is on a long journey that eventually brings Him to Jerusalem. The Gospel of Mark is similar. Jesus called people to a journey by faith. What does it mean to journey by faith? Frederick Buechner says, "Faith is stepping out into the unknown with nothing to guide us but a hand just beyond our grasp."[1]

Follow Me—I Know What I'm Doing

Jesus also is saying, *Follow me because I know what I'm doing.* Jesus knew Who He was and what He was doing with life. This Man could say, *I do always those things that please the Father.* I can't say that. Can you?

There is a relation between being and doing. In this Man, being and doing were united in perfect tandem. In Him we see what human life is supposed to be. As the model person, Jesus was the paradigm of God's new humanity. Jesus was what God has in mind for all of us, that personhood toward which we journey.

But emulating Jesus doesn't mean we lose our own identities. People discover when they are following Jesus that they are most truly themselves. Christ never does obliterate our personalities, never colors us all gray. Following Jesus just enhances our own uniqueness.

Jesus enables us to realize our selfhood because He accepts us just as we are. Christ takes whatever gifts we bring to the task, accepts them, and blesses them. While each of us is called to witness, Jesus never demands that we all do it the same way.

I suppose there is nothing surprising about a belted kingfisher being on the lookout for fish. God has equipped him to be a fisher. But the musical song sparrow witnesses to God in other ways by warbling his melody from the treetops. The plumed cardinal makes its appeal to our sense of beauty with the crimson flash of wings against the evergreens. All of them witness to their Creator. We are called to follow and to bring along for service on the journey whatever talents we have at fishing, or singing, or making beauty.

It's a wonderful thing how many different models for witnessing the New Testament gives us. In the book of Acts, there is some form of the word witness 21 times. The reader is left without any doubt of the intentions of the writer of Acts, "You will be my witnesses" (Acts 1:8).

Life comes to us with its opportunities, and we respond in the ways in which we are gifted. God expects all of us to witness, but He expects us to use our own gifts in that witnessing.

Let's identify several models for witnessing which use different gifts. One of them we could call the *confrontational* model. Jesus modeled this for us with the rich young ruler. *You only lack one thing. You are very close. One thing can be everything, and you need to set this one thing right.*

Jesus was also confrontational when he dealt with the Pharisees in Matthew 23. The confrontational mode of witnessing is direct and often planned. It's the mode we use when we take a prospect card and go out to witness, perhaps to a total stranger.

There is another witnessing approach, which we could call the *cultivative* model. It's deliberate and gradual. Jesus modeled this with His disciples. He cultivated them over a period of years and gradually taught them many things.

There is the *confessional* model. This is the tell-your-own-story kind of witnessing. It's what the man in John 9 was doing when he said, *All I know is that once I was blind and now I can see.* It's what the Gadarene demoniac did after he was healed. He wanted to go with Jesus and Jesus said, *No, you stay home here and tell your story to the folks who know you best.*

There is also the *relationship* model of witnessing. We all have relationships. This model is a personal witness to friends or acquaintances as the opportunity arises. Take Zacchaeus; Jesus wanted to go home with him for lunch. He did, and through His witnesses Zacchaeus experienced conversion. Zacchaeus underwent some kind of conversion as Jesus took the time to relate to him. We all have relationships.

There is the *spontaneous* model of witnessing. It's not planned at all. Witnessing was never intended to be a parenthesis. Jesus found opportunities for witnessing within the day. They came to him unannounced. It is the approach he used with blind Bartimaeus of Jericho, and the woman who touched Him in faith, and with the woman at the well.

Jesus was a master at the *indirect* form of witnessing. Look at His parables. His parables are such beautiful and oblique stories. He comes in the side door or the back door before we know it.

There is a *scriptural* witness. We have all known people who cannot quite get tongue and mind in gear but they are committed to handing out the Scriptures and tracts. What a beautiful form of witnessing! Jesus loved to quote the Scriptures. Look at the Gospel of Matthew and note how many times the Scriptures are quoted.

There is the *ministry* model of witnessing. This is the cup-of-cold-water approach where some ministry opens the door for a testimony. That's what Southern Baptists are doing when we feed the world's hungry people. That's what happened to Norm and Beverly Coad, my dear friends, who served the Lord in Burkina Faso for years, distributing food to starving people, only to be invited by the Muslim country of Mali to come in and serve there.

I don't find a single instance in the New Testament where Jesus makes any distinction between evangelism and ministry. I never find one time when Jesus says, *I've been doing ministry, now I am getting ready to do evangelism.* Where did we get that division? For Jesus it was all one bolt of cloth.

Certainly these eight models overlap. But they were all modeled by our Lord, they are all valid, and have all been used successfully

I believe the weakness of every witnessing clinic I have ever attended was that it attempted to set up one way to witness as the norm for everybody. Jesus puts the lie to that. *Follow me, I know what I'm doing, and with me you will know what you're doing too.*

Follow Me—And Be Ready to Sacrifice

Jesus also says, *Follow me and be ready to sacrifice.* Each disciple gave up something to follow Jesus. And for what? For cross bearing.

Have you ever felt you were on a cross? Does that surprise you? I have a dear pastor friend who was talking to me several years ago about some rough times he had had in his church and how mistreated he felt. And he said, "You know one day I came to the sudden realization that I really expected to be treated better than Jesus was."

Jesus was up-front. He offered no cheap grace at bargain-basement, cut-rate prices. When Jesus gave an invitation it was hard to walk down the aisle. When He said take up your cross and follow me, it was a lot more than metaphor.

Look at the metaphors in this focal passage from Mark 1. First the metaphor of journey, one of the great metaphors of the Scriptures. We are on a journey toward the new Jerusalem, toward the future.

Fishing is another metaphor. "Follow me, . . . and I will make you fishers of men." Surely another metaphor that is here at least by implication is homecoming. What a powerful metaphor! Aliens, pilgrims, sojourners, on a journey trying to get to a better land, a better home. Why is the metaphor of homecoming so compelling? Perhaps the answer is in the quote by Meister Eckhart, the mystic; "God is at home, and we are in the far country."[2]

Christ calls on every one of us to live sacrificially in following Him. But we can't sacrifice what we don't have. He called fishermen to become fishers of men, but we have no evidence that He called tax collectors the same way. Our calling is related to our gift. What happens when Christians follow their gifts? They are at their best for the Lord in the kingdom, in the church, when we let them give what they have to give without demanding something else from them. Jesus knew that good fishermen would make good fishers of men.

Fishing is a highly individual thing. No two fishermen go about it the same way. It's a matter of style, choice, and gifts.

Follow Me—I'm on My Way to the Future

Jesus was radically future-oriented. He had little interest in the past. He never did inquire of His disciples, "Who are you, and where have you been, and what have you done?" Jesus was interested only in what they might yet do out in the future.

Jesus called people to a journey, not to a theology. Never once in the New Testament did Jesus define what it means to be His disciple in terms of what a person believed. He called people to a mission, not to a creed. He never gave any qualifications for being one of His disciples except the willingness to follow Him.

He tells them right up front that following Him means some changes. He is going to make them become something greater than before. They are going to become fishers of men. Becoming is what discipleship is all about. We do not "become" instantly. We follow instantly, but we do not "become" instantly. It takes a while.

Jesus holds us accountable for a willingness to change, to become. Have you noticed how few folks want to really change? Folks want to get fixed. But they don't want to change. Unfortunately, Ernest Campbell is right when he observes that the church is usually the obstacle to change unless it takes special precaution to be otherwise.[3]

Follow Me—Now

Jesus is also saying, *Follow me now.* In verse 18 they left their nets immediately. Great decisions are made in an instant. The tragedy of the unseized moment is known to every one of us. Psychologists say every time we fail to act on good intentions immediately, the chances are we will never act on them.

Albert Schweitzer in his great book on the historical Jesus wrote: "He comes to us as one unknown without a name. As of old by the lakeside he came to those men who did not know him. He speaks to us the same word, follow thou me. And sets us to the tasks that he has to fulfill for our time. He commands. And to those who obey him, whether they be wise or simple, he will reveal himself in the toils, the conflicts and the sufferings which they shall pass through in his fellowship. And as an ineffable mystery they shall learn in their own experience who he is."[4]

Called to follow, accountable to become. Good fishing calls for concentration and single-mindedness. We will see people "caught," snatched from the powers of evil, added to the kingdom, and brought into the full life of the church when we too have but one thing on our minds.

Disciples: Called to Follow, Accountable to Become

When Jesus began to seek followers, He didn't go to the masses. He went one by one to a small group of men. They were for the most part a rather unpromising band—fishermen and tax collectors. Who would have thought they could turn the world upside down? (Acts 17:6).

Just the Facts

God continues to call ordinary people. He calls us to follow. Often we hear of a call to preach or to be a missionary. The first call, however, is to follow, and it comes to all who will listen. The roles we fill may change through the years, but the call to follow endures.

The invitation to follow Christ came to one Romanian woman in a worship service. While she was well-educated and successful, something was missing in her life. The congregation consisted of simple, uneducated folks. It had been impossible for Christians to receive a college education during the Communist regime, and these people had paid the price. As the visitor looked around her, however, she became increasingly aware of the congregation's depth of commitment and her own great need for Christ. She felt guilty and unclean. Peace, love, joy, and purpose became hers as she committed to follow the Christ served by these simple people. Regardless of station in life, the call to follow is the same.

Beyond the Facts

After following Jesus long enough to discover that His way was not always easy, some of His disciples dropped by the wayside. "You do not want to leave too, do you?" Jesus asked the Twelve. Simon Peter answered him, 'Lord, to whom shall we go? You have the words of eternal life'" (John 6:67-68).

Today we follow Christ not because of the physical comfort He promises but because of the eternal life He offers.

The call to follow is not an end in itself; it leads us to a commitment to serve. For many the commitment leads to service in faraway places, requiring separation from family and living in uncomfortable situations. God's call is demanding and competes with the world's demand for ease, comfort, and wealth.

Seldom, however, are we asked to risk life and limb. Our risk in following Christ more often involves touching the untouchable, loving the unlovely, reaching out to those who need God's love and acceptance. But we don't know how to minister to those in need; for the most part, we don't even *want* to know how to minister to those in need. We think we can't afford to contaminate our fellowship with people we deem social and moral misfits.

In Spite of the Facts

Jesus, however, was quick to reach out to touch the lepers, the sick, the dying, even though in the Jewish tradition it caused Him to be considered unclean. He ate with sinners and challenged cynics. He spoke to outcasts and washed His disciples' feet. He gave bread to the hungry and hope to the hopeless.

Your call to follow has placed you in the process of becoming like Him. What is He asking you to risk? Visiting a woman in prison? Feeding the homeless? Teaching someone to read? Giving hope to a pregnant teenager?

It's so comfortable just to come to worship services and hear God's word, fellowshipping with people just like yourself. But God calls us to the world, to be salt and light.

Write in your notebook what ministry and witness He is calling you to accept.

How will undertaking this make you a better disciple? Ask Him to give you courage and vision to become all He wants you to be.

Pray this prayer: "Disturb us, O Lord, when we're too pleased with ourselves; when our dreams come true because we dreamed too little; when we have arrived in safety because we have sailed too close to the shore.

"Disturb us, O Lord, when with the abundance of the things we possess, we have lost our thirst for the water of life; when having fallen in love with time, we have ceased to dream of eternity. And in our efforts to build the new earth, have allowed our vision of the new heaven to grow dim.

"Stir us, O Lord, to dare more boldly, to venture on wider seas where storms shall show Thy mastery and, where losing sight of the land, we shall find the stars. In the name of Him Who pushed back the horizons of our hopes and invited the brave to follow, even the name of Christ Jesus our Lord. Amen."[5]

---

[1]Frederick Buechner, *The Magnificent Defeat* (New York: Seabury Press, 1968), 99.

[2]Annie Dillard, *Holy the Firm* (New York: Harper Colophon Books, 1977), 62.

[3]Ernest T. Campbell, "Continuity and Change," in *Christian Manifesto* (New York: Harper and Row, 1970), 93.

[4]Albert Schweitzer, *The Quest of the Historical Jesus* (New York: Macmillan Co., 1964), 403.

[5]Tim Norman, pastor of Ginter Park Baptist Church, Richmond, VA; commissioning prayer by Dellanna O'Brien, August 1989.

10

Easter People: Called to Believe, Accountable to Tell Others

Focal passage: John 20
Focal verses: John 20:21,29

The New Testament material about the resurrection comes from several sources. Each of these sources tells something unique. For instance, the sermons in the first five chapters of the book of Acts tell us that the earliest church merely preached the resurrection. They didn't try to explain it; they just preached it.

Then, a few years later, in 1 Corinthians 15 for instance, which dates from around A.D. 55, Paul introduces into the growing Easter tradition a list of Resurrection appearances made by our Lord.

A few years later, the Gospel of Mark introduces the first empty tomb narrative as the tradition grows, as the data is gathered, as the story is fully known.

In the Gospel of Luke, perhaps written in the A.D. seventies, Luke includes detailed narratives of Resurrection appearances. There wasn't just an empty tomb, but the Lord appeared to people. Luke gives some of those details. Then in the late eighties or early nineties, Matthew comes along and comes closer to actually narrating the Resurrection itself than any other Gospel. He combines what Mark had given, the empty tomb, with what Luke had given, resurrection appearances, and he puts the two together in one place and then goes on to give us that marvelous Great Commission about going into all the world and discipling people.

Finally, in the last decade of the first century, the Gospel writer John gives the most fully developed Resurrection material. He elaborates on the empty tomb. He gives more Resurrection appearances than any other Gospel writer. He also gives us Peter's commission to lead this new church movement.[1]

It is with this Fourth Gospel, the Gospel of John, that we are concerned as we think about the Easter people in John 20. According to John, Jesus died on Passover eve, Nisan 14, just before the beginning of Sabbath at sundown on Friday night. On Sunday morning during the fourth watch, between 3:00 and 6:00, Mary Magdalene came to the tomb.

Interestingly, in all four Gospels, Easter begins with the women visiting the sepulcher. The last ones to leave His cross Friday afternoon were the first ones to come to His tomb Sunday morning. Where were the men? It wasn't the last time that question would be asked in the church. The women were at the tomb on Easter morning. They came back to the source of their grief.

In John 20 there is a subtle play between seeing, believing, and knowing. I count some 14 references to *seeing* or *saw*. There are 7 references to *believing*, and 4 references to *knowing*. These form a subtle triangle. John raises the question, Is seeing believing, or is believing seeing? He tells us about Easter people who are called to believe and accountable then to go tell others what they've seen and what they've believed.

What Do You See?

The first Easter person that we meet is Mary Magdalene

(John 1:1-10). In John's Gospel Mary Magdalene first comes to the tomb on Easter morning. We can study these verses in terms of what was seen. (Remember that *see* is one of John's key ideas in this chapter.)

What Mary saw when she got to the tomb on Easter morning was the stone rolled away (John 20:1). But Mary drew her own conclusion and ran off to find Simon Peter and the beloved disciple. She reported to them not what she had seen, but her interpretation. What was that interpretation? "They have taken the Lord out of the tomb, and we don't know where they have put him" (John 20:2).

How did Mary get from the rolled-away stone at the tomb to the conclusion that somebody had stolen the Lord's body? By interpretation. All of us are interpreters. We interpret what we see, hear, and need.

Interpretation is never simple. The listening ear always manages to distort the spoken word. The seeing eye, the observing eye, always shapes and forms what it sees. Interpretation is at work everywhere. The stone was rolled away, but Mary concluded that somebody stole the body.

An old Chinese adage has it that two-thirds of what we see is behind our eyes. Of course, two-thirds of what we hear is between our ears, so it's important that behind our eyes and between our ears we have something with which to work. The truth gets run through our mental filter and so it always gets interpreted.

Some people say they don't believe in interpreting the Bible. They say: I just take the Bible and read it like it is and that's that. That sounds good and it preaches great, but the truth is that nobody does just that. The Scriptures have to be interpreted. Most of us can't read the Scriptures in the original languages. We're dependent on a translation, and translation always involves interpretation. Even punctuation involves interpretation.

Be wary of learning the Bible from people who say they aren't interpreting it. Some people have such a strong need for authority that they believe their favorite preacher or teacher doesn't interpret the Scriptures, just repeats and passes on the exact mind of God. Our interpretation of the Bible will never be any more enlightened than we are. If we believe in witches, or if we believe in the irresistible power and presence of demons all around us, or if we believe in snake handling in worship or baptism for the dead, or faith without any medicine to make us well when we're ill, we'll find all of that in the Bible. It's all there. Interpretation of the Bible is always necessary, and it's never simple.

The same Holy Spirit who inspired this Bible that we love so much promises to help us interpret it. God promises to help us understand it. Whatever else the Bible may be, it is literary. Whatever else the Holy Spirit may be, He is literate.

Mary saw a rolled away stone and she interpreted that to mean somebody had stolen the Lord's body.

Now enters the second Easter person, Simon Peter. He got to the tomb on Easter morning after a footrace through the streets. He went into the tomb impulsively (just like we'd expect Peter to). What did he see? Linen burial clothes lying in one place. Across the way lay the napkin headpiece that had been wrapped around the head of the Lord, rolled up neatly and set aside.

This suggested to Peter that the body hadn't been stolen but that something else had happened. As far as we can tell from the record in John 20 Peter saw only these linen napkin clothes and concluded that, obviously, the tomb was empty. That was Peter's interpretation of the evidence.

The emptiness of the tomb in and of itself doesn't say anything. How do we get from an empty tomb to the persuasion that Christ is alive? No evidence is here that Peter believed with resurrection faith simply because he found the tomb empty. So enters the third Easter person.

He is called throughout this Gospel "the beloved disciple." He is never named. Traditionally, we have believed he was John. He got there first, allegedly because he was younger. After the footrace with Peter he arrived at the tomb first, but not being quite as impulsive as Peter, and perhaps considerably younger, he didn't enter until Peter got there. He stooped and looked in.

Later, after Peter had gone into the tomb, the beloved disciple did enter. Verse 8 is important. He entered, saw, and believed. There's a big difference between the way this disciple sees the empty tomb and the way Peter saw it. This beloved disciple was the first believer in a resurrection. Without the appearance of an angel, or the resurrected Jesus standing in front of him, without even so much as a proof text, because they didn't yet know the Scriptures, this disciple saw the empty tomb and he believed. His faith was dependent on neither sight nor the Scriptures. His faith was an event out of his own inner life.

Peter had seen the same things at the tomb that morning that the beloved disciple saw, but as yet we have no indication that Peter believed. Getting there first was no advantage because Peter brought nothing with him to the emptiness of the tomb. He had no expectations, and so he saw nothing but an empty tomb.

Two-thirds of what you see is behind your eyes. The empty tomb by itself doesn't necessarily produce faith. It didn't for Mary, for Peter, or for the other disciples.

But for the beloved disciple, the empty tomb was a sign of something else. Not only was Jesus not there, but He was also risen. "He saw and believed" (John 20:8).

Now the question starts to come into focus. Is seeing believing? Or is believing seeing? Facts alone never command faith. No one finally becomes a Christian because the evidence is so compelling that he or she cannot do otherwise. Miracles don't automatically produce faith. John makes this point over and over again. Why? Because miracles can always be interpreted some other way.

So what do you see in the emptiness? What do you conclude from the empty places in life? You may have been in those empty places. You may be there today. Both nature and spirit abhor a vacuum. Something is there that doesn't like an emptiness, that wants to rush into the empty places of life. As the beloved disciple stepped into the empty tomb on Easter morning, something in the emptiness around him called out to the emptiness within him. When emptiness calls to emptiness faith may just be in the making.

Rusty was a child with Down syndrome. Things usually went badly for Rusty. The other children laughed at him. The

Sunday School teacher did her best to include Rusty in the class, but it was never easy.

In just seven months Rusty would die. Today, however, was Easter, and Rusty was in Sunday School with the other children. The teacher had carefully prepared her lesson and her learning activity. She gave each of the children a plastic egg. Then she sent them out into the bright spring morning to look all around the churchyard for something symbolic of Easter to put in the egg and to bring back to class. She told the children to come back in ten minutes and they'd talk about it. So they did.

One child brought back in his plastic egg some fresh blades of green, spring grass. Another one caught a colorful butterfly. A third child found a spring flower.

Everyone watched as Rusty brought his egg back into the class. Sure enough, as expected, when he opened it, there was nothing in it at all. The other kids began to snicker.

And Rusty said: "But don't you see, don't you see, it's empty?"

I Have Seen the Lord

What do you see in the emptiness? In John 20:18 Mary could finally say, "I have seen the Lord." Still weeping, Mary stayed at the tomb, stooping to look in, and what did she see? Two angels sitting there.

But Mary wasn't impressed. She was interested in her Lord. That's what she came looking for; she hadn't found Him, and angels didn't impress her in the least. Mary wasn't resigned, and she stayed at the tomb, still connecting the empty tomb with "them," who must have taken away the Lord's body.

In verse 14 something dramatic begins to happen. Mary for the first time looks into the face of the resurrected Jesus. "At this, she turned around and saw Jesus standing there, but she did not realize that it was Jesus." She saw, but she didn't know. Is seeing believing or is believing seeing? She looked into Jesus' face and mistook Him for the gardener. Mary didn't expect to see Jesus, so she didn't see Him.

Jesus then asked Mary the same question the angels had asked: "'Woman,' he said, 'why are you crying? Who is it you are looking for?'" Mary still didn't recognize Him even after He spoke. *Here's the gardener*, she thought. Look at the evidence that Mary had. She had seen the empty tomb, the grave clothes, the headpiece, two angels, and now Jesus Himself. She saw Him, but she still had no Resurrection recognition or faith. Evidence alone doesn't produce faith.

In verse 15 *they* becomes *you*.

"'Sir, if you have carried him away, tell me where you have put him, and I will get him.'" What a moment! As Mary stood between an empty tomb that hadn't impressed her but only intensified her grief and a living Christ that she didn't yet recognize, the most dramatic thing of all happened. The Lord spoke her name and finally got her attention.

"Mary."

She turned and said, "Rabboni," (which means Teacher)" (John 20:16).

There is such a wide variety in the way people come to faith. For the disciples it came only after Jesus showed them His hands and feet and side. Thomas needed to touch the wounds. The men on the Emmaus road had their eyes opened when He broke bread with them. But for Mary, it was the calling of her name. We all come to faith in a different way.

Look at verse 17. Jesus said to her: "Do not hold on to me, for I have not yet returned to the Father. Go instead to my brothers and tell them, 'I am returning to my Father and your Father, to my God and your God.'"

Mary was now given a mission. She was made accountable for what she had seen and heard. *Go to my brothers.* Well, why weren't the brothers there to see for themselves? Why didn't they linger a while at the tomb and ponder all this?

Jesus entrusts the original Easter message to this woman, Mary Magdalene. In the Jewish world, the testimony of a woman wasn't highly valued or trusted. Mary couldn't have testified in any Jewish court of law. She may have had a sordid and suspect past. She'd come from a notoriously wicked village, Magdala. At one time, she'd been possessed of seven demons. There was every reason in the world to doubt Mary's testimony. And Jesus entrusted to her the most momentous news in the spiritual history of mankind. Mary, by all human standards, wasn't qualified to proclaim it.

When she found the brethren, she said, "'I have seen the Lord'" (John 20:18). But first we know she heard Him call her name, "'Mary.'" This is a beautiful passage, which speaks of the priority of hearing the word. She'd seen all kinds of evidence and it hadn't persuaded her. But when she heard the Lord, then she believed.

The Disciples Were Glad—When They Saw

Now enter more Easter people. "The disciples were overjoyed when they saw the Lord" (John 20:20). Is seeing believing, or is believing seeing? We read in these verses that the disciples were gathered together, but we also read some other things. First, the doors were locked and they were gathered in fear. As long as locked doors and fear prevail, the church won't be able to go on mission. This isn't what Jesus intended for His church. They were gathered (that's to their credit), but fearful and behind locked doors.

Jesus appeared to the disciples with His greetings of peace, a fulfillment of the promise He made in chapter 14. "I will not leave you as orphans; I will come to you. . . . Peace I leave with you; my peace I give you" (John 14:18,27). He showed them His hands and His side, and we read in John 20:20 the disciples were glad when they saw the Lord.

Then in the next verses Jesus gave them three other things. First, He gave them a mission. He made them accountable. "I am sending you" (John 20:21).

Next, He gave them the Holy Spirit (John 20:22). This is called the Johannine Pentecost. Jesus breathed on them. The Holy Spirit came by insufflation. It's a different kind of account from what Luke gives in the book of Acts. Maybe it was a temporary filling with the Holy Spirit to get them to Pentecost for the great missions launching event. I don't know, but He gave them the Holy Spirit.

Then He gave them authority to proclaim the forgiveness of sins (John 20:23).

Thomas had missed being with the disciples one week before on Easter evening when Jesus had come. He wasn't there.

Maybe he had given up in despair. We don't know. But it's plain what happened. Thomas missed Sunday night church. So he missed seeing the Lord. He was not convinced the next week by the testimony of all the brothers. Every one of them said, *Thomas, I tell you we saw Him, He was there, He was as real as you are.*

But Thomas said, *No amount of evidence is going to convince me until I can see and touch because seeing is believing.* Thomas was skeptical, cynical, and disillusioned. He was the original empiricist. He had been burned. *I've got to see for myself. I've got to touch in order to believe.*

Some people are just as hard and skeptical as Thomas. But Jesus doesn't withdraw even from the literalism of such folks as this. The crude and narrow empiricism of such people doesn't put Jesus off. Jesus gave Thomas another chance. Isn't our Jesus the Lord of another chance?

The following Sunday the group was together again, this time with Thomas. Jesus isn't afraid of skepticism. I believe our Lord must have understood somehow that faith without doubt is dead. Doubt is the cutting edge of faith, the growing frontier. We need our Thomases in the church. Let's not draw the net so tightly that there is no room for the occasional Thomas among us. Our Thomases keep the rest of us honest.

The doors were still shut. They'd seen the Lord, but they weren't ready to open the doors, which suggests it takes more than one week to get the church to open up even after God stages a resurrection. But Jesus came anyway, and He brought a peace greeting once again (John 20:26).

Then Jesus issued His challenge to Thomas. *Alright, Thomas. Seeing is believing; perhaps seeing and touching are believing. So go ahead and touch my hands, if you will. Put your hand in my side, Thomas. It's alright, go ahead.*

And Thomas shrank from this invitation, saying, "My Lord and My God."

Some New Testament texts imply that Jesus was God, such as Colossians 1:15. There are some other texts that probably refer to Jesus as God, such as 1 John 5:20.

But at least three verses of Scripture explicitly call Jesus God. Hebrews 1:8-9 says, "But about the Son he says, 'Your throne, O God, will last for ever and ever.'" And John 1:1, "In the beginning was the Word, and the Word was with God, and the Word was God." And this verse, John 20:28, is the clearest example, "My Lord and My God."

This confession represents the mature New Testament expression of faith. It is the high point of the Gospel of John, and confessionally the high point of the whole New Testament. Who makes that confession, but this old skeptic, cynic, empiricist, Thomas. Jesus noted that while it's blessed to see and believe, it's also blessed to believe without seeing.

Each of us is called and each of us is accountable. We haven't called on God, but He has called on us and appointed us to go forth and bear fruit that abides. We are called to venture and accountable to obey along with Abraham and Sarah. We are called to a life of wonder and accountable to be faithful even while we wonder along with Mary and Joseph. We are called to follow. We are accountable to become. Like all of Jesus' disciples, we are called to believe and accountable to tell others because we too are Easter people.

Easter People: Called to Believe, Accountable to Tell Others

Did you ever wonder where you would have been during the time of Jesus' Crucifixion and Resurrection? Would you have been with the women who remained at the cross and then went early in the morning to the tomb? Or would you have fled in fear as did Peter and others? Would you have shared John's assurance that Jesus had truly arisen? Or would you have been more likely to doubt, as did Thomas? Where would you have been among the Easter People?

"Surely," we might say, "if I personally heard the testimony of John and Peter and Mary, I would believe." But in the story of Lazarus and the rich man, Jesus said that if we do not believe the prophets of old, neither would we believe if one should come from the dead (Luke 16:31). What then causes one to believe and confess and another to deny and reject?

Just the Facts

Pastor Daniel Lee of the First Korean Baptist Church of Silver Springs, Maryland, in comparing the differences between Korean and American Christians, maintains that they result from the differing worldviews. Koreans come from an animistic background where the supernatural is accepted and expected. Therefore, it is easy for them to believe that God hears and answers prayer. Americans, on the other hand, haven't grown up with an appreciation of the mystical and have a great deal of difficulty believing in supernatural power. What then can bring us to belief in Christ?

Beyond the Facts

For many of us, belief in Christ was the result of nurturing of Christian parents and a church family. The modeling of the Christian life and the expression of genuine love exemplified in a Christian family testify to a loving heavenly Father.

Some of us came to believe Christ through the testimony of a friend or family member. Others found Him in the pages of the holy Word. For some, only through the valley of deep despair and tragedy were you able to find the compassionate and forgiving Christ.

Just now, review the circumstances of the first time you said, "Yes, Lord, I believe."

Write your memories in your notebook. Thank Him, once again, for His mercy and love.

In Spite of the Facts

Salvation isn't meant to be cherished and preserved, however, but to be celebrated and shared. The woman at the well was compelled to go and tell all those in Sychar, that she had met One Who told her all the things she had done. Could He be the Messiah? (John 4:29).

When Peter and John were instructed by the Jerusalem Council not to speak or teach in the name of Jesus, they responded, "For we cannot help speaking about what we have seen and heard" (Acts 4:20).

If we live by the same values and principles Jesus and His disciples had, reaching out to others with the message of salvation is natural. It becomes a life-style, not a project. We see others, not as interruptions, but as persons needing to hear about Christ's love. Every encounter becomes a divine appointment, a prearranged meeting in which we see the needs, the loneliness, the despair, and we are empowered to bring hope and peace through Jesus Christ.

Is there an urgency within you to go and tell? If not, consider the priorities in your life. Are they in keeping with the confession of Paul, "For to me, to live is Christ"? (Phil. 1:21) Have daily concerns and ambitions replaced spiritual growth in competing for your energies and gifts? As beneficiary of eternal life, we are obliged to share the good news with others.

In all honesty, list the true priorities of your life. Are they godly priorities? Ask God to help you arrange your priorities according to His will for you.

Many of us would like to tell others about Christ, but we lack the skill in telling. Larry Taylor has told us in chapter 9 that there is no single way to witness; instead there are many ways. He describes eight models: confrontational, cultivative, confessional, relationship, spontaneous, indirect, scriptural, and ministry. Within these models all of us can discover at least one way we can share the message of Christ.

Review the description of the models and select one which you feel comfortable using. Identify one person in your life who needs a witness and begin praying for him or her. As the Holy Spirit leads you, pray for courage to be obedient. Open yourself to be used to bring the Easter story to someone else. Many wait to hear, some who will never know unless you tell. Join the Easter people in singing, "Alleluia! Christ is born in human hearts. Christ is risen indeed!"

---

[1]Reginald H. Fuller, *The Formation of the Resurrection Narratives* (New York: Macmillan Co., 1971), 1-145.

Section 3

Servanthood

11

The Servant of the Lord

Focal passages: Isaiah 42:1-4; 49:1-6; 50:4-9; 52:13 to 53:12
Focal verse: Isaiah 52:13

Servanthood is a central theme in the prophecy of Isaiah, and we turn in this chapter to perhaps the greatest of the Old Testament prophetic books. How can we even think about missions and the church and our calling to carry the message of Christ without thinking of servanthood? And where better to begin the study of servanthood than with Isaiah?

The word *servant* (*ebed*) appears about 40 times in the entire book of Isaiah, but the term appears frequently in chapters 40 to 55, the great second section of Isaiah, set in the sixth century B.C. during the Babylonian exile. In these 16 chapters the word *servant* appears 21 times. Most of these references are clearly to Israel.[1]

However, in four passages the servant figure is unique, and questions about the servant of the Lord in those passages have fascinated scholars for centuries. These four passages are 42:1-4; 49:1-7; 50:4-9; and 52:13 to 53:12. To understand the biblical background of the servant theme we must start with these four passages.

We need to first recognize the kind of literature included in these Isaiah passages. The four Isaiah passages that speak uniquely of the servant of the Lord are poems or hymns. These four servant poems are among the most disputed passages in all the Old Testament. Scholars have a terrible time agreeing on them.[2] Perhaps the main reason these poems are so difficult is that while Isaiah tells us the work of this servant of the Lord, he doesn't tell us the servant's identity.

In 1892 an Old Testament scholar named Bernard Duhm identified these four servant poems as self-contained units which stand apart and which merit careful consideration on their own. They are unique to Isaiah and without real parallel anywhere else.[3]

Behold My Servant

Our first stop en route to an understanding of Isaiah's servant figure is chapter 42, verses 1-4. Yahweh, God of Israel, presents the servant to some unspecified audience (Isa. 42:1). There follows a brief description of the servant and his task, which is to establish justice. He will accomplish his task in a quiet, unassuming way (Isa. 42:2-3). The two metaphors in verse 3 are a poetic way of saying that the servant will act so gently that even the weakest of people won't be hurt. There may be a slight hint of his suffering in verse 4, a feature that comes out strongly in the later servant poems.

This first of the four servant poems introduces the figure of the servant. From the beginning he is a mysterious figure. The first servant poem is closely related to its context in the previous chapter of Isaiah (41:8-10). Already we begin to see some of the essential features of this servant of the Lord. He works for justice, he goes about his tasks without fanfare, and he expects to suffer.[4]

A Light to the Nations

The second servant poem is found in Isaiah 49:1-7, and it expands the picture of the servant. In this poem we hear directly from the servant himself, who said nothing in the first poem. The servant claims that God called him from his mother's womb (Isa. 49:1) and gave him a unique gift of com-

munication (Isa. 49:2). The servant has been given an aggres-
sive work to do (Isa. 49:2) and he is carefully concealed by
God until the appropriate time. In verse three the servant is
identified with Israel—the only place this occurs in the four
servant poems. His task is a mission to Israel. He is to glorify
God. Verse four is a lament by the servant in which he
mourns his ineffectiveness but returns to an assurance he is
grounded in God.[5]

The second servant poem takes a turn in verses five and
six. His mission is expanded by the Lord to include all the nations. The servant will be a light to the nations so that God's
salvation reaches the ends of the earth.

In this second poem the person and the mission of the servant become much clearer. This poem stands entirely apart
from its context. We get a glimpse of the servant's frustration
over the failure of his mission. This mission has to do with
communication.[6] It is a mission of Israel to be the servant to
all the nations. Our understanding of the servant grows in
this poem. Servants, it seems, have missions involving some
communication, they can expect frustration and suffering,
and their mission as servants of God is to all nations.

The Gift of Speech

The third servant poem is found in Isaiah 50:4-9. Once
again the servant speaks in first person (Isa. 50:4). The
tongue given to him by God is mentioned, another reference
to his message and his task of communication. God's gift to
him is the power of His word to sustain the weary. There are
two references to teaching. The servant is a teacher, and also a
learner (Isa. 50:4). The servant's intimate relation to Yahweh
is described. He is a disciple of Yahweh whose mission involves the spoken word (Isa. 50:5).

However, the servant experiences opposition, even violent
opposition (Isa. 50:6). Again the theme of suffering and persecution is sounded. His suffering is finally vindicated as the
Lord proves to be trustworthy and powerful (Isa. 50:7-9).

The picture of the servant of the Lord is expanded even
further in the third servant poem. The emphasis on learning
and teaching, the mission of word and message, the reality of

violent persecution, and the steadfastness of the Lord all bring
further focus and clarity to the image of the servant.[7]

My Servant Shall Be Exalted

The fourth servant poem is incomparably the greatest and
best known of the four poems. Indeed, it is one of the greatest
passages in all the Bible and is even regarded by many as the
high watermark of the Old Testament.

This fourth poem begins in Isaiah 52:1*b* and continues
until the end of chapter 53. The poem both begins and ends
with speeches by God describing the servant's greatness and
faithfulness. The first divine speech reveals two startling
things about the servant, one of which is entirely new in the
four poems. His appearance is terribly disfigured (Isa. 52:14).
"Just as there were many who were appalled at him—his appearance was so disfigured beyond that of any man and his
form marred beyond human likeness."[8]

The second surprise about the servant is that he will
"sprinkle" many nations, or make sacrifice or purification for
many. The verb in verse 15 is *yazzeh,* which often means "to
sprinkle"; and that seems to be its meaning here. The
disfigured servant will make sacrifice, or sprinkle, nations,
hence the surprise of the kings (Isa. 52:15).[9]

The servant had insignificant beginnings, with much suffering and pain (Isa. 53:1-3). His contemporaries even
thought his affliction must be a punishment from God (Isa.
53:4). But the speakers came to the shocking realization that
the servant suffered not because of his own sins but for the
sins of others (Isa. 53:4-5). This understanding represents the
most profound concept of suffering in all the Old Testament.

There is something noble and impressive about this servant's suffering. He suffers quietly and silently through his ar-
rest and persecution (Isa. 53:7-8). His death at last is
ignominious (Isa. 53:9). The fourth servant song ends with
another divine speech (Isa. 53:11-12). While there is no ex-
plicit statement of a resurrection, the servant will know a
great reward in the future (Isa. 53:12). The servant's interces-
sion for others is mentioned four times in verses 11 and 12.[10]

In these four poems Isaiah gives us one of the Old Testament's greatest figures. He raises as many questions as he answers about the servant of the Lord. We search the pages of the Old Testament in vain looking for someone who fulfilled the servant image. Like many of the great promises or figures of the Old Testament, this servant became one of Israel's deferred dreams, idealized and projected onto the future, waiting for the day when God's perfect servant would at last arise.

Of Whom Does the Prophet Speak?

In the eighth chapter of the book of Acts we read about an Ethiopian eunuch travelling in his chariot on the way home after worshiping in Jerusalem. Philip the evangelist joined himself to the chariot and discovered that the eunuch was reading from the prophecy of Isaiah, the fourth servant poem in chapter 53.

Philip asked the man if he understood what he was reading, and the man said, "'How can I,' he said, 'unless someone explains it to me?'" (Acts 8:31). So he invited Philip to join him in the chariot. After reading Isaiah 53:7-8 together, the Ethiopian man asked Philip the timeless question that readers of the servant poems have been asking ever since. "'Tell me, please, who is the prophet talking about, himself or someone else?'" (Acts 8:34). Philip began with this very Scripture verse and told this man the good news of Jesus.

What an appropriate question: "Of whom does the prophet speak?" Isaiah gives us strong ideas about the servant's work, but he never tells us his identity.

The term *servant of the Lord* is ambiguous. Down through centuries of biblical interpretation there have been two main approaches to the identity of the servant. The first approach is the collective interpretation. It's the oldest interpretation and it notes that the servant of the Lord in Isaiah always appears in close identity with the nation Israel. Isaiah frequently uses the term *servant* to denote Israel's relationship to God. There is no doubt that Isaiah saw Israel's role among the nations as that of a servant.[11]

However, this interpretation of the servant as the nation Israel is fraught with difficulties. For one thing it is impossible to identify Israel's lack of faith and her unwillingness to obey

God with the self-sacrifice of Isaiah's picture of the servant of the Lord. At no point did Israel ever conceive of herself as servant to the nations. Israel felt she had been chosen by God for privilege rather than for service. Servanthood has never come easy for the people of God, and it still doesn't. We are somehow reluctant to be the world's servants.[12]

Another version of the collective interpretation suggests that perhaps the servant was the faithful servant mentioned several times in Isaiah (10:19-22; 11:11,16; 28:5; 37:32). This might seem more plausible except for the fact that in all four servant poems the servant is depicted as an individual.

So the collective interpretation of the servant as the nation Israel is not without its problems. Yet it does have support for several reasons. First, Isaiah 49:3 does explicitly say, "You are my servant, Israel." Second, the context of the four servant songs is the whole book of Isaiah, which speaks often of Israel the servant. Finally, there is the concept of corporate personality, developed by the great British Baptist scholar H. Wheeler Robinson and others which notes that among the Jews one individual can represent the whole group, or clan, or nation. Hence the individual language of the poems could still embody Israel the nation as the servant.[13]

The second interpretation of the servant is that he is some individual in Israel's history. But this raises the question of whether Isaiah envisioned the servant as past, present, or future.[14]

Many fanciful interpretations identify the servant as some figure in Israel's and Isaiah's past. There is a striking similarity between the suffering servant and Deuteronomy's picture of Moses. Moses is referred to in Deuteronomy as God's servant 36 times. Both Moses and the servant act as mediators between God and Israel, both suffer, and both finally die for the sins of the nation.

Several other individuals roughly contemporary with Isaiah have been suggested as the model for the servant. Jeremiah, Job, and Isaiah himself have all had their advocates.

Still another possibility is that Isaiah envisioned some individual yet to come in the future of Israel, perhaps long after Isaiah's prophecy was history.

Once again, though, all the various individual interpretations have their drawbacks. Not only does Isaiah apparently identify the servant with Israel, but no single individual ever came up to Isaiah's picture of the servant. The Jewish mind was never capable of thinking of a suffering messiah, and besides, the messiah was an idealization of the king, not the nation.[15] For all these reasons a pure individual interpretation of the servant is now ruled out by most Old Testament scholars.

What are we to make of the servant? The most recent, and perhaps the best, interpretation of the servant is the fluid approach which says that the figure of the servant in Isaiah's poems fluctuates within the four poems. Sometimes the servant is the nation Israel, while other times he is a futuristic individual. This approach retains the strong features of both interpretations and avoids the weaknesses. The suffering servant is best understood as Israel at its ideal in the form of one person.[16]

What Does the Servant Do?

Here we are on much surer footing. We can see what Isaiah's servant does. Isaiah gives us the most profound interpretation of redemptive and vicarious suffering to be found in the Old Testament. If we focus now on just the fourth servant poem (Isa. 52:13 to 53:12), we can see the vocabulary of pain and suffering stretched almost to the breaking point. This servant who suffers contradicts the old orthodox theory of suffering as always punitive, as punishment for sins.

In the fourth servant poem we see the picture of perfect innocence suffering for the guilty. The use of pronouns in Isaiah 53:4-6 heightens the contrast between the servant and the rest of us. Look at the powerful language of suffering in the verbal forms of these verses: *stricken, smitten, afflicted* (Isa. 53:4); *pierced, crushed* (Isa. 53:5); *oppressed, afflicted* (Isa. 53:7); *cut off, stricken* (Isa. 53:8).

What, then, does the servant of the Lord do? First, he suffers voluntarily and in silence (Isa. 53:7). There is a quiet dignity in silent suffering. It requires immense self-control to be silent under unjust treatment. The quiet endurance of wrong can be an impressive and compelling thing.

Patience under trial certainly wasn't common among Old

Testament sufferers. Jeremiah knew great suffering, and Habakkuk also, but neither of them was silent. We speak commonly of the patience of Job but anyone who has read Job knows he howled and screamed in his misery, as we all would.

Isaiah's servant is unique. He stands alone as a silent sufferer. That may be why his spiritual nobility is so marked.

Second, Isaiah's servant suffers completely. He suffers all alone and apparently without reason. Some scholars feel that the servant is pictured as a leper. The verbs that describe his suffering are heavy: *despised, rejected, stricken, smitten, afflicted, pierced, crushed, oppressed.*

Third, the servant suffers by design (Isa. 53:10). God is doing something even in this extreme suffering.

Fourth, the servant suffers vicariously. Note Isaiah 52:6, "the iniquity of us all." *Many* occurs in the fourth servant poem four times (Isa. 52:14,15; 53:11,12).

In the New Testament there are three powerful metaphors to describe the atonement of Jesus: sacrifice, substitute, and victor. The sacrifice metaphor was borrowed from the altar, the substitute metaphor from the law courts, and the victor metaphor from the battlefield. Strikingly, all three metaphors occur in Isaiah 53: sacrifice (Isa. 53:10), substitute (Isa. 53:4-5), and victor (Isa. 53:12).[17]

Fifth, this servant suffers victoriously. There is an undeniable note of triumph despite the gross suffering. Instead of an air of defeat there is the air of triumph.

Who Is the Servant of the Lord?

There has never been any real question in the mind of the Christian about the true identity of Isaiah's servant. Where, we might ask, in all of history is there such a figure as his? Only one person fits Isaiah's portraits of the suffering servant. Only once has Israel produced such a servant. The New Testament writers picture Jesus as the fulfillment of Isaiah's prophecy. What Israel failed to accomplish as a nation, Jesus gloriously achieved, just as Isaiah promised. There can be little doubt that the influence of the servant ideal is on every page of the New Testament.

In the next chapter our task will be to draw the connection clearly between the New Testament's account of Jesus the Servant and Isaiah's Old Testament picture of the suffering servant of the Lord.

The Servant of the Lord

"He wants me to be what? A servant? You've got to be kidding! I've spent my life trying to be really somebody, and now you think I'm going to become a servant? Forget it!"

"I can't imagine what got into Mary. She had this expensive jar of perfume, and she rubbed it all over Jesus' feet. What a waste! Why, it could have been sold for at least 300 denarii and given to poor people!"

"And then after supper he did the most amazing thing. He took a basin of water and began to wash our feet. All conversation ceased. We could not believe it! The Master, washing our feet!"

How is it ever possible to explain to the world the concept of servanthood? Most titles given Jesus were straightforward and apparent: Son of man, King of kings, Lord of lords, Master, Rabbi, Light, Bread. But Suffering Servant?

Just the Facts

Raisa Ivantsova lives in the Ukraine, part of the Commonwealth of Independent States, formerly the USSR. The negligent nuclear accident in Chernobyl released huge amounts of radiation into the atmosphere. She developed leukemia. Treatment in the US, provided by caring doctors and loving friends, has brought remission for now. But Raisa faces an uncertain future. Raisa suffers because of the negligence of men.

Patrick Daly, beloved principal at PS 15 in the rough Red Hook section in Brooklyn, had earned the love and respect of the students in his school and their parents. Constantly providing support and encouragement, he effected change in the entire community. Recently, while visiting in the neighborhood of one of his students, he was shot unintentionally in a gangland battle. He and the entire neighborhood have suffered because of the evil of men.[18]

Many examples can be given of the suffering brought about by the actions of others. Unfortunately, such events are quite common. Finding a case where someone suffers for another, deliberately and vicariously bearing another's pain, is a much rarer occurrence, however.

Beyond the Facts

Occasionally, we read in the newspaper that someone has given a kidney or bone marrow to a victim of renal failure or cancer. Because this kind of sacrifice is rare, it is newsworthy. There are even those who have given their lives in order to save a child or another loved one. When the stakes are high enough, then such a sacrifice is deemed appropriate.

Jesus said: "Greater love has no one than this, that he lay down his life for his friends. You are my friends if you do what I command. I no longer call you servants, because a servant does not know his master's business. Instead, I have called you friends, for everything that I learned from my Father I have made known to you" (John 15:13-16).

The Suffering Servant was willing to give all for the sake of His friends. He "took up our infirmities," "carried our sorrows," "was pierced for our transgressions," and "crushed for our iniquities." Amazing love.

In Spite of the Facts

Christ, the Suffering Servant, provided the ultimate model for servanthood. He came not to be served, "but to serve, and to give His life as a ransom for many" (Mark 10:45).

Some years ago a film was made of the life of Edith Vaughn, a longtime missionary in Brazil. Dedo Weigert, gifted photographer from Germany, did the filming.

After several days of observing Edith at work, Dedo could no longer hold back the question: "Miss Vaughn, why do you do this? Why would you put up with the opposition of some of the people and run the risk of being harmed?"

Edith's beautiful blue eyes sparkled. "Why, that's easy," she said. "'For there is no other name under heaven given to men by which we must be saved.' These people must know that."

In God's kingdom, servants serve. And so must we.

Record in your notebook a time when someone, out of Christian love, was a servant to you. What did the experience teach you?

How has the Lord called on you to be a servant? Have you accepted that call with humility and love?

Has the Lord called on you to suffer for His sake? If He did, would you be willing to do so? Pray for the kind of faith that is operative regardless of circumstances. Who knows when you might need it?

---

[1]Robert R. Ellis, "The Remarkable Suffering Servant of Isaiah 40-55," *Southwestern Journal of Theology* 34 (Fall 1991): 20.

[2]Ibid.

[3]Ibid.

[4]Ibid., 21.

[5]Ibid., 22.

[6]Ibid, 23.

[7]Ibid.

[8]Ibid.

[9]Ibid., 23-24.

[10]Ibid., 24.

[11]Ibid.,25.

[12]Ibid., 26.

[13]Ibid., 25.

[14]Ibid., 26-7.

[15]Ibid., 28.

[16]Ibid., 28-29.

[17]J. S. Whale, *Victor and Victim* (Cambridge: University Press, 1960), 46.

[18]*Birmingham News,* Friday, December 18, 1992.

12

The Lord Who Was a Servant

Focal passages: Luke 22:24-27; Philippians 2:5-11
Focal verse: Luke 22:26

Some of the most exciting Bible study we can do is to take a biblical idea and follow its development through the Scriptures. Servanthood is such an idea that rewards the careful Bible student. Few concepts in the Scriptures have a longer or nobler history than servanthood.

In the Old Testament Moses is called "the servant of the Lord" 36 times. The prophets expanded the idea of servanthood, each in his own way. Amos was a rasping voice for God in the eighth century B.C. among a people with no social conscience. Hosea suffered his way to servanthood through domestic heartbreak. Jeremiah wept his way to greatness as God's servant in the sixth century B.C.

Isaiah's suffering servant, however, registered the high watermark of servanthood in the Old Testament. Isaiah writes of an innocent servant who suffers completely and vicariously for the sake of others. The reader of Isaiah's servant poems is left with little doubt about what the servant does. The only question is to the identity of this servant.

Like so many of the great Old Testament images, the servant of the Lord was an ideal picture or symbol that was never achieved in the Old Testament.

Then a man appeared, so unique and having such a profound impact on the lives of his countrymen, that one by one the old idealized images were resurrected and applied as titles to this man, Jesus of Nazareth.

One of the oldest such images applied to Jesus was the servant of the Lord. Throughout the Bible there is a reduction of focus from the whole creation to the nation Israel, to a faithful remnant, and finally to a single man, Jesus.[1]

Servant of God is one of the oldest Christian titles for Christ. The Jews never could accept the idea of a suffering messiah. Jesus had to redefine messiah. He had to swim against the popular current of Judaism to define Himself to His followers.

Probably the identification of Jesus as the Servant of the Lord was made by Jesus Himself. Luke never connects the suffering servant with Jesus, nor does Matthew ever refer to Isaiah 53 in connection with Jesus. While John does refer to Isaiah 53 and its suffering servant, in all likelihood it was Jesus Who found His identity in the Old Testament Scriptures by combining two great images, or deferred dreams: the son of man (Daniel) and the suffering servant (Isaiah).[2]

It is conspicuous that the various gospel writers make only marginal connection of Jesus with the servant of the Lord, particularly as seen in Isaiah. There is, in fact, only one quote from the fourth servant poem by Jesus Himself (Luke 22:37). Some scholars think that something in the early church kept the writers from making more extensive use of this image from Isaiah.[3] Whether that is the case, it may have been at His baptism that Jesus knew for certain that He was at last the Suffering Servant of Isaiah come in flesh to redeem His people.[4]

A Dispute over Greatness

The question of Jesus' identity over against the image of the servant is not settled by counting the number of quotes in the New Testament from Isaiah's four servant poems. It is settled best by listening to Jesus' teaching and by watching His behavior. Jesus taught service by word, deed, and being.

In Luke 22 a dispute arises among Jesus' disciples as to who is the greatest of them. The greatest, of course, was among them, but this wasn't a dispute over Jesus' greatness; they were talking about themselves.

In this respect the disciples as yet are no different from the rest of the world. The world devises elaborate ways of deciding who is the greatest. Our society has an insatiable need to determine number one, to crown the most beautiful, to identify the 100 richest (i.e., greatest).

To the extent that the church lives the same way and haggles over the same things, we are no different from the rest of the world (Luke 22:23).

The broader context of Luke 22 makes this dispute over greatness seem even smaller. It is the eve of Jesus' Crucifixion. In the very shadow of the cross the disciples argued over who was the greatest. In less that 24 hours Jesus would establish greatness for all times by becoming the Suffering Servant of the Lord on the cross, "pierced for our transgressions" and "crushed for our iniquities" (Isa. 53:5).

So, with far more urgent matters no doubt on His mind, Jesus had to take time out once again to teach about greatness. He did this by setting up a contrast or a tension between the way things are in the world and the way they are to be among His people (Luke 22:25).

Kings among the Gentiles exercise lordship and those in authority exercise control. Such is the nature of the world and its institutions. The important words here are *lordship* and *authority*. There is only room in the church for one Lord, and all authority belongs to Him. Only one Lord understands that greatness and authority have to do with servanthood.

The little "church" Jesus had gathered about Himself didn't yet understand that. One suspects that the much bigger church now gathered doesn't yet understand it either.

It must have been discouraging to Jesus to see on the eve of His Crucifixion that the disciples as yet had not grasped what His work and mission were all about. How much more discouraging it must be to Christ today to see that we haven't progressed much in the church even yet. We still dispute among ourselves such things as greatness and authority.

Luke 22:26 is stark and forceful. *But not so with you.* Jesus puts down a knife blade, as it were, between the world's obsession with greatness and how things are to be among His people.

Unless the church learns how to be different in the world, a new humanity living by a code set apart from the world's code, the world is simply going to continue passing the church by as irrelevant.

"'But you are not to be like that. Instead, the greatest among you should be like the youngest, and the one who rules like the one who serves.'" In Jewish society the youngest in a family would be expected to be second to the oldest. Jesus calls for the leader to be the one who, like the youngest, is expected to serve. What the church needs now is leaders who are willing to be servants and servants who are willing to lead. As long as the laity draw their models for leadership from the business community and the civic club rather than the example of Jesus, and as long as pastors accept these alien models, the church will continue to haggle over authority and greatness as Jesus goes to the cross.

In this passage the marvelous arithmetic of Jesus becomes apparent. His was a singular calculus the world has never understood and the church has understood only occasionally.

In Jesus' arithmetic the usual values and standards are reversed. *But not so with you.* Less becomes more, the least becomes the greatest, losers are winners, and the servants are the leaders. In the world, "who is greater, the one who is at the table or the one who serves? Is it not the one who is at the table?" (Luke 22:27). We may expect the world to be concerned about who sits where at the table. We may expect the world to define greatness as rank, position, power, wealth, success, and authority. *But not so with you.*

Those who follow Jesus are to be different. If the salt loses its flavor, and the light is hidden, and the leaven withheld from the loaf, where is the world to find its flavor, its light, and its leaven? In the ones who lord it over the rest and seek only to clarify the parameters of their own authority? Admittedly, the church can take on all the appearances of power and success by following the world's lead. Theologian H. Richard Niebuhr noted, "Christendom has often achieved apparent success by ignoring the precepts of its founder."[5]

"But I am among you as one who serves." Jesus is among us, not at the head of the table, but waiting on the table. Look for Him out in the kitchen with the servants. The vast humility of God is found in the vast humanity of Christ, the Servant. Myron Madden imagines that in heaven we are all going to be shocked to learn that God is the most humble person in the universe. Chaplain Madden pictures God as being among all the beings in heaven, Himself incognito. Our task will be to figure out which one is God after talking to everyone present.[6] "But I am among you as one who serves." Unless we look in the church among the servants we won't see Christ.

The New Testament picture of Jesus is of the Teacher, the Prophet, and, most of all, the Servant. If we would see Jesus in His church, we must look for Him where He is.

The Form of a Servant

There is no way to do justice to Philippians 2:5-11 in a few pages, or in 100 pages for that matter. This may be Paul's greatest passage. It is a magnificent hymn to Christ, poetry of the highest theological order. I had an English professor who said, "The poets know more about God than the theologians." What I've come to discover is that the best poets are theologians, and the best theologians are poets. Paul is both poet and theologian in this passage and few have ever surpassed him in either category.

Paul spoke often of the mind of Christ. "Your attitude should be the same as that of Christ Jesus" (Phil. 2:5). "But I am among you as one who serves" (Luke 22:27). *Have this mind among yourselves.* The two verses dovetail nicely. Both of them are speaking of servanthood. *This mind* is the mind of service, the only mind that is appropriate in the Lord's church.

This mind is one we have *in Christ Jesus.* Paul's favorite phrase is one he uses more than 150 times. To be in Christ is to know Him, His mind, as our own, as our very environment. We are in Christ as a fish is in water, as a bird is in the air. Jesus modelled humility and servanthood for us in that, "Who, being in very nature God, did not consider equality with God something to be grasped" (Phil. 2:6).

The entire passage turns on this sentence. Paul is saying that Christ was of the same nature as God. Since He already had this affinity with God, it might have been natural for Him to aspire to equality with God. This would have been to reject the way of humble obedience and to choose another path. Christ wasn't tempted by an opportunity which the rest of us would have found irresistible. The point seems to be Jesus' humble obedience to a way that would lead to suffering.[7]

Jesus chose another course, and that is Paul's point. The kings of the Gentiles lord it over their subjects, but not so with you (Luke 2:25-26). We are to choose another course. With the mind of Christ among us we will resist any temptation to grasp at equality with God, and we will go the way Jesus goes. Christ emptied Himself, taking the form of a servant, being born in the likeness of men (Phil. 2:7).

Instead of aspiring to an even higher status, Jesus gave up what He had. He laid aside the divine privilege and privacy that go along with being in the form of God, and took on Himself instead the form of a servant. Here in this verse Isaiah's servant of the Lord, Jesus' own teaching about servanthood to his disciples, and Paul's sublime poetry about the servant Jesus, all converge.

The scholars have debated the meaning of the words *emptied Himself* and haven't agreed. Of what did Christ empty Himself? One interpretation has it that He emptied Himself of His divinity. This view has it that the preexistent Christ made a decision to lay aside temporarily some of the prerogatives of divinity in order to assume humanity. This view is known as the kenotic interpretation from the Greek word for emptying, *kenosis*.[8]

Another interpretation suggests that what Paul has in mind in these critical verses (Phil. 2:6-8) is somewhat less than Christ's temporarily laying aside His divinity. It would interpret the decision made by Christ to be strictly an earthly decision rather than a preexistent one. It says that the emptying was not the surrender of Christ's divinity but the acceptance of servanthood. Nowhere else in the early church is it asserted that Christ made a preexistent decision. The incarnation is best understood as *epiphany,* which means manifestation, rather than *kenosis,* emptying.[9]

Regardless of which of these views we take, the point seems clear enough. Jesus knew humility and obedience, and He knew it by choice. He chose the way of servanthood, and that point provides the obvious connection between Paul's servant hymn here in Philippians and Isaiah's servant figure in his four poems.

The divine humility and obedience led Christ to a cross, not to a throne on the earth (Phil. 2:8). The progression in Philippians 2:6-8 is striking: "the very nature of God" (Phil. 2:6), "the very nature of a servant" (Phil. 2:7), and "appearance as a man" (Phil. 2:8). This beautiful hymn has a certain plot, a story design to it. Like the classic story it starts out with everything well (Phil. 2:5-6), followed by a dramatic change or decline which eventually bottoms out (Phil. 2:8), and then it starts up again toward some resolution (Phil. 2:9-11). The cross is the low point in the hymn, and paradoxically also the high point. It is precisely because the divine servant chose the obedient route which led to a cross that He is now exalted (Phil. 2:9).

The action in this hymn parallels the action in the fourth servant poem in Isaiah, where the servant of the Lord plunges to the depths of suffering, only to be at last raised to greatness (Isa. 53:12). Indeed, it might well be that Paul's mind moved from Isaiah's servant, through the experience of Jesus, to this profound hymn of the Christ.[10]

In his exaltation God has given Christ Jesus a new name, probably the name Lord (Phil. 2:11). Lord was the Resurrection title for Jesus. The giving of a new name in the Scriptures is meaningful. Sarai became Sarah. Abram became Abraham. Jacob became Israel. Jesus became Lord. A unique value is attached to a name in Jewish thought. To give one's name was to give one's self. A person was believed somehow to be present in his name. Much is made in the Old Testament about God's name. The changing of a name is a significant event.[11]

The result of this change in name is such that every knee

will bow to creation's Lord. The idea seems to be that Christ has obtained through obedience the very thing He refused to grasp, that is equality. There follows one of the Scriptures' great confessions. The Bible is a book of great confessions of faith, and Phil. 2:11 is one of the greatest.

There can be little doubt that the theology of this passage is some of the loftiest in the New Testament. It must be remembered, however, that Paul's purpose here is practical. He is working against the feuds and jealousies in the Philippian church, and encouraging Christian people to rise above such things by an appeal to the servanthood of Jesus.[12]

The scriptural motif of the servant finally comes around full circle. Moses was the servant of the Lord. Isaiah pictured a suffering servant. Jesus taught servanthood as true greatness and washed His disciples' feet. Paul memorialized in divine poetry the servant path chosen by Jesus. The message comes through everywhere—Go and do likewise, the servant is not above his master, and have this mind among yourselves. For true greatness, for genuine leadership, the church has never found a better way than the form of a servant.

The Lord Who Was a Servant

We live in a day of marvelous technology. Human organs are transplanted from one body to another—hearts, kidneys, corneas. How truly remarkable it would be if we could experience an attitude transplant, in which the mind of Christ would replace our own, so that all our thoughts, our hidden musings, our candid reflections, our deliberate plans—all were from Christ's mind, not ours.

Just the Facts

God's plan, believe it or not, was just that. When His Holy Spirit takes up residence in our lives He transfers the thoughts and desires of the Father into our own hearts and minds. If we are faithful to yield ourselves to Him, He will make His attitude ours. Paul writes, "For it is God who works in you to will and to act according to His good purpose"

(Phil. 2:13). Not only will the Holy Spirit urge our commitment to servanthood, He will also equip and enable us to do whatever He asks. Charles Finney has said, "If God commands something, that is the highest evidence that we can do it."[13]

Beyond the Facts

Larry Taylor has told us that the disciples who follow Jesus are to be different. In the Philippians passage, Paul identified three characteristics of a servant of Christ.

1.Obedience. Oswald Chambers says it beautifully: "The best measure of spiritual life is not ecstasies but obedience."[14] When serving a master, nothing substitutes for obedience. What does obedience in your life mean? Are you willing to say, "Yes, Lord"?

2.Selflessness. Christ emptied himself until all that was left was servant. We, on the other hand, measure out our service like doses of medicine. Many in our world today are caught up in the desire for wealth.

Peter Marshall said, "It is so difficult for us to transfer our affections to things above, for we have fallen in love with toyland, and our playthings are so dear."[15]

What are some things you hold too dear?

3. Humility. Few people outside Christ would value this quality. Our Lord, however, exemplified humility often, nowhere more beautifully than when He took the towel and basin and washed the feet of His disciples. F. B. Meyer has said, "I used to think that God's gifts are on shelves one above the other and that the taller we grew in Christian character, the more easily we should reach them. I find now that God's gifts are on shelves one beneath the other and that it is not a question of growing taller, but of stooping lower and that we have to go down, always down to get His best ones."[16] The sheaves of wheat with the heaviest fruit bow the lowest.

Christ's servants are obedient, selfless, and humble.

Read the Philippians passage once again, paying special note to the three qualities of servanthood. Look for examples of these qualities in your own life. Identify those times in your recent past when you were disobedient, selfish, or proud. Ask God to forgive you and to give you a servant heart.

In Spite of the Facts

The servant nature causes us to go counter to the normal response of society. How long has it been since someone has seen in you the unique qualities of a servant?

Review the questions and answers in your notebook thus far. How have you grown during this study? Sometimes growth is painful, sometimes joyful. Jesus came as a Servant. How will you now serve Him?

---

[1]Oscar Cullmann, *The Christology of the New Testament,* trans. Shirley C. Gutherie and Charles A. M. Hall (Philadelphia: Westminster Press, 1959).

[2]Ibid., 64-69.

[3]James Flamming, "The New Testament Use of Isaiah," *Southwestern Journal of Theology* 2 (Fall 1968): 99.

[4]Cullmann, *The Christology of the New Testament,* 66-67.

[5]H. Richard Niebuhr, *The Social Sources of Denominationalism* (New York: Meridian Books, 1929), 3.

[6]Myron Madden, *Claim Your Heritage* (Philadelphia: Westminster Press, 1984).

[7]Ernest F.Scott, "The Epistle to the Philippians, Introduction and Exegesis," in *The Interpreter's Bible,* ed. George Arthur Buttrick (Nashville: Abingdon Press, 1956), vol. 11, 48.

[8]Frank Stagg, "Philippians," in *Broadman Bible Commentary,* ed. Clifton J. Allen (Nashville: Broadman Press, 1971), vol. 11, 196.

[9]Ibid.

[10]Scott, "The Epistle to the Philippians," 49.

[11]Ibid., 50.

[12]Ibid., 52.

[13]Albert M. Wells, Jr., ed., *Inspiring Quotations* (Nashville: Thomas Nelson Publishers, 1988), 143.

[14]Ibid.

[15]Ibid., 128.

[16]Ibid., 92.

Section 4

Involvement

13

Invitation to Involvement

Focal passage: John 1:19-51
Focal verse: John 1:39

The Gospel of John begins in mission. The Word comes from eternity, from God into history on mission. John the Baptist is also sent from God on mission with all the authority to speak for God. Later in the Gospel Jesus insists that He is sent from God. Mission permeates the Gospel of John from start to finish.

In this chapter we're studying avenues of involvement. God in Christ seeks to win us to Himself by all means; that is, He spares no effort. Once God has our attention, He invites us on a mission.

Ways to Tell a Story

There are two classic ways of telling a story. One way is the way Mark does it in his Gospel using the messianic secret. At the end of Mark a lone centurion stands before the cross and says, "Surely this man was the Son of God." Only at the end do we know for sure Who Jesus is.

There's another classic way of storytelling. In the Gospel of

John it pleased the Holy Spirit to use that other means. In the Gospel of John we are told in chapter one the most important thing in the whole book. The Word became flesh. In the opening verses of chapter one John tells us what he has to tell us, and then spends the rest of the book substantiating it.

This way of telling a story is almost like a movie flashback. We already know the secret from the beginning. However, this is a difficult way to tell a story because if you tell your readers the secret at the start, how are you going to hold their attention for 21 chapters?

John knows he has this problem and he addresses it skillfully. John keeps our attention with conflict, irony, misunderstanding, and metaphor. This makes it possible for John always to communicate on two levels. He too has a surprise ending. It's called resurrection.

John's Negative Witness About Himself

In chapter 1 John the Baptist offers a negative witness to himself in verses 19-28. In these verses the authorities from Jerusalem have come to ask him, *Who are you?*

John began by telling them who he was not. There's a sense in which all witness to oneself must be negative witness in the light of Christ. Or, as John puts it later in the gospel (John 3:30), "'He must become greater; I must become less.'"

John, the Gospel writer, is getting ready to show us the witness of various people to Jesus, and he starts with John the Baptist. Jesus' enemies were already gathering testimony against Him. From the beginning of the Gospel of John, Jesus' trial has already begun. We usually think of the trial occurring at the end of His life, but not in John's Gospel. The trial is already underway from chapter 1 and the authorities from Jerusalem have come to John the Baptist to subpoena his testimony as evidence against Jesus. After they've collected all the evidence to be found, they're going to kill Him.

John begins by telling who he is not (John 1:20-21). He gave these inquirers a triple negation of himself. These three denials become progressively more emphatic. They ask him who he is and he doesn't deny, but confessed in verse 20, "'I am not the Christ.'"

Well, the authorities say, *we can check that one off. He says he isn't the Christ. Well, then, who are you?* They continue the interrogation. "Are you Elijah?" The Jews expected Elijah to come back again.

More emphatically John said, "I am not" (John 1:21).

Let's ask him one more question. Are you perhaps the prophet?

The Jews universally believed that in the last days another prophet like Moses would come, according to Deuteronomy 18:15. So perhaps this John the Baptizer was the prophet of the end time, the prophet like Moses.

In the most emphatic of his three denials John said, *No, I am not the prophet of the end time.* John disassociated himself from any of the great figures which the Jews expected at the end of time. They looked for the Christ; they looked for Elijah; they looked for the Mosaic prophet; and John said, *I'm not any of these.*

There's a sense in which the Old Testament is a book of deferred dreams. In the Old Testament the king was an important figure. As every new king came to the throne, the people said, *Ah, this is the man. This is the ideal king we've been waiting for. He will lead Israel to her appointed destiny.*

With the ascendancy of every new king the people were disappointed. Over the centuries there developed this idea of the perfect king. It became a dream and was deferred to the future because no historic king ever fulfilled the dream. When the last kings were finally led off to Babylon in chains, Israel had a dream deferred.

This dream became the hope for the Messiah about which we read in Isaiah (chaps. 9 and 11). What do we find when we get into the Gospels? Every one of them shows Jesus as the fulfillment of the deferred dream of the perfect king.

We meet other ideal figures in the Old Testament that were projected onto the future as deferred dreams. There was the son of man (Daniel), wisdom personified (Prov. 8-9), the ideal high priest (like Melchizedek and David), and the suffering servant of the Lord (Isaiah). Israel's dreams were greater than her history. All these figures, including the messiah and the prophet of the end time, awaited fulfillment. In the New Testament every one of these dreams is applied to Jesus.

So, naturally when John the Baptist appeared people associated him with some of these ideal figures. John, however, denied that he was any of them.

In John 1:23 John tells them who he is. "John replied in the words of Isaiah the prophet, 'I am the voice of one calling in the desert, "Make straight the way for the Lord.""" So John identified himself with past, present, and future. He identified with Scriptures, particularly Isaiah 40. He positioned himself with the prophets.

The Pharisees asked how he justified his actions (John 1:24-28). For the first time Jesus' enemies were identified by name. These Jews from Jerusalem are called Pharisees. John told them not to be surprised at his baptism, not to overestimate it. It's only water baptism, he said. The scandalous thing about what John the Baptist was doing was that he was baptizing good Orthodox Jews. That never happened before. Only proselytes experienced water baptism.

John said in John 1:26-27, as he moved toward his first testimony to Jesus, Who is still unnamed, "'I baptize with water,' John replied, 'but among you stands one you do not know. He is the one who comes after me, the thongs of whose sandals I am not worthy to untie.'" Four things John said about Jesus, still unnamed. First, *The one to look for already stands among you.* Second, *You don't know him.* Third, *He's the One Who's coming after me.* And fourth, *I'm not even worthy to be his slave.* Already Jesus is for John an avenue of involvement which unites the great past of his people with the future of God's new activity.

John's Positive Witness to Jesus

John has just given a negative witness of himself. He's ready now to give his positive witness concerning Jesus (John 1:29-34). We had four negative denials; now we have four positive affirmations. Here's the first one (John 1:29): "Behold the Lamb of God who takes away the sin of the world."

Here we have another great title for Jesus, the Lamb of God. The figure of the lamb occurs everywhere in the Old Testament and in Jewish life. It's a complex idea and it isn't entirely clear which lamb from the Old Testament John has in mind when he applies this beautiful metaphor to Christ, the Lamb of God.

Is he talking about the cultic lamb sacrificed at the temple every day? That's the first possibility. Is he talking about the scapegoat or the victim lamb that bore the sins of the people away into the wilderness on the Day of Atonement (Yom Kippur)? That is the second possibility. A third possibility is that John was thinking about the Paschal Lamb slain at Passover and eaten in memory of the Passover and the Exodus from Egypt. A fourth possibility is that John has in mind the beautiful picture from Isaiah of the Suffering Servant as the lamb dumb before his shearers, smitten, stricken, and afflicted of God. A fifth possibility is that he is thinking about the apocalyptic ram so prominent in the apocalyptic literature such as the book of Revelation.[1]

None of these five provides the precise antecedent of the Lamb Who takes away the sins of all the world. Probably what John has in mind here is the Paschal Lamb that was slain at Passover because later John comes back to this theme subtly. Jesus is actually crucified on Passover eve just as the Paschal Lambs are being slain in every household all over Palestine. It's a powerful symbol.

The first positive affirmation of Christ, in John 1:29, was "Look, the Lamb of God." The second one, "A man who comes after me has surpassed me because he was before me," occurs in John 1:30.

Usually in Judaism any time a person followed another religious leader he was considered subordinate to that leader. But John insists that coming after him there is One Who is before him not only in rank but in existence. Any time this kind of language is used in the Gospel of John he is talking about the preexistence of Christ. This is the apex of New Testament Christology.

These early Christians knocked the ends out of time and eternity. They said in order to understand the Christ event we must go back to eternity itself. This is a reference to the preexistence of Jesus.[2] Later on in this Gospel, Jesus says not only was he before John the Baptist, "before Abraham was born, I am!" (John 8:58).

The third positive affirmation John gives to Jesus is in John 1:32: "'I saw the Spirit come down from heaven as a dove and remain on him.'" Here John draws a sharp contrast between mere water baptism, such as he had done, and baptism in Holy Spirit, such as Jesus would do. In other words, in Jesus, flesh and spirit are permanently united. It's the primary way God involves Himself with us. Every avenue of involvement in God's mission in the world requires us to embody Christ for someone.

In John 1:34 we have the fourth positive affirmation that John gave to Jesus: "'I have seen and I testify that this is the Son of God.'" These titles for Jesus are being piled one upon another. In the Gospel of Mark, these titles would come out slowly and gradually, but in the Gospel of John they are all in chapter 1. Son of God is one of the great titles for Jesus in the New Testament. It has a rich Old Testament background. In the Old Testament this title of Son of God was applied to three groups: to kings; to special emissaries on mission; and occasionally to the entire nation of Israel as sons of God.

Jesus is certainly a king, and He is on mission from His father, and finally He represents everything that Israel ever dreamed. He was Israel's deferred dream finally come true. From the start of the Gospel of John, Jesus is on mission. His mission outlines the mission of others. Jesus' mission in the world involves everyone who acknowledges Him.

The Witness of the First Disciples

That brings us to John 1:35-42, the witness of the first disciples. John is writing on two levels—a historical level, and a theological level. On this third day, as Jesus walked by, John the Baptist was standing with two of his disciples. One of them is Andrew, the other one isn't named.

John said once again, "Look, the Lamb of God." Hearing this, these two disciples left their master and started following Jesus. John knew he was running that risk. He knew he was about to lose two of his most faithful disciples. But a greater one than John had arrived. The avenue of involvement for these two disciples was to be Jesus, not John.

As Jesus walked along He was aware someone was following Him. He turned to look at these two former disciples of John the Baptist, and Jesus asked them a question (John 1:38): "What do you want?" *What are you looking for?* It's one of the great questions of the Bible and it is Christ's question to us, to every would-be disciple. Jesus' first words in the Gospel of John are a question, and it's a question that touches the nerve of our own involvement in mission: *What are you seeking? What is it you're looking for?*

The two disciples said, "Rabbi, where are you staying?" They responded with a question of their own. *We just want to be where you are. So where are you staying?*

John is the only Gospel to make extensive use of the title Rabbi, and John interprets it in the text. It means teacher. Fifty-nine times in his Gospel, John gives these little interpretative remarks off the cuff. In the first half of the Gospel of John the disciples call Jesus Rabbi, but in the second half they call Him Lord.

When these two disciples followed Jesus and asked where He was staying, John is using one of his favorite verbs translated as *abiding, remain,* or *stay.* It is the verb *menein,* which we have seen before. It has to do with the permanence of God among us, and it has to do with John's theology of immanence, where the Father and the Son and the believer are all in intimate fellowship. It's similar to Paul's great term *in Christ.*[3] To be in Christ is to be staying where Jesus is.

In response to the disciples' question, what does Jesus say? He offers them a magnificent invitation. He says, *Come and see.* Here is Jesus' all-embracing challenge to faith. In the Gospel of John the noun *faith* is seldom if ever used. John doesn't use the noun *pistis* (faith), but John describes faith with verbs and he does it in three ways.

The first way is coming to Jesus. The second way is seeing Jesus with perception. The third way is believing in Jesus. When John wants to describe faith, he uses one of these verb forms: *coming* to Jesus, *seeing* Jesus, or *believing* in Jesus. Jesus' great invitation to these disciples is, *Come and see.*

Jesus invites these two disciples, and all would-be disciples today, to come with Him and just see what happens. It's an invitation without coercion to anybody that's open-minded enough to follow. It's one of the great invitations of the Scriptures, the avenue that leads us to further involvement with God's mission in the world.

Jesus appeals to us by all means. One of those means is invitation to pilgrimage.

Dean Alan Jones of the Grace Cathedral in San Francisco says that God has fallen in love with us and wants us to come home.[4] This journey is a pilgrimage expressed here in the simplest terms. It's your invitation and mine. Come and see. If we journey long enough, where do we arrive? We arrive at God, only to discover that God's been with us all along in Jesus.

Jesus' invitation is an opportunity to allow God to change our drifting into pilgrimage. Drifting is aimless, pilgrimage is a journey with purpose.

In his beautiful Christmas oratorio "For the Time Being," W. H. Auden pictures the three wise men from the East journeying as they follow the star. Each wise man has an opportunity to speak and tell why he's making this trip. The first one says, "To discover how to be truthful now is the reason I follow this star." The second wise man explains his journey like this: "To discover how to be living now is the reason I follow this star." The third wise man says, "To discover how to be loving now is the reason I follow this star."

Finally all three wise men summarize their journey like this: "To discover how to be human now is the reason we follow this star."[5] What the world needs now are real human beings animated by the spirit of Jesus.

The Bible tells us three things about ourselves, all of them in the opening chapters of Genesis. We are creatures made out of dirt. That should forever keep us humble. Second, we are made in the image of God, which means that we are addressable by God. Third, we are sinners. The first two things were done by God. He made us as creatures. He made us in His image. But the third thing we did ourselves. We became sinners.

The definition of what it means to be human is to be a creature in the image of God. Where is one? Jesus was the only One ever willing to be what God made us all to be. Why,

He didn't think it was robbery to grasp after equality with God. Consequently, He didn't have to. He took on the form of a servant and submitted Himself to all of the weaknesses of the flesh. To be human is to be Christlike.

These two disciples were so excited they ran off to make other converts. Andrew went on mission to his brother Simon Peter and he said, *We have found the Messiah.* All of this took place out of church. You can witness out of church!

David Buttrick says, "Evangelism is to gossip faith in secular places."[6] We'd better learn how to gossip faith in secular places. If we follow the avenue of involvement that Jesus opens to us, it will lead us into engagement with the world.

What is this journey that we've talked about? First, it is an invitation to come home. T. S. Eliot wrote:

> We shall not cease from exploration.
> And the end of all our exploring
> Will be to arrive where we started
> And know the place for the first time.[7]

This journey is an invitation to venture. When you venture, there's always risk.

This journey is an invitation to go on mission. We cannot walk up to the Lamb of God and look at Him and turn away and not go on mission. Mission is our avenue of involvement in the task of bringing all people to Christ. So Andrew brought his brother, Simon Peter, the fruits of his mission, to Jesus.

Philip brought Nathanael later to Jesus. Nathanael was so impressed with Jesus because Jesus already knew him before he got there. Nathanael said, "How do you know me?" (John 1:48).

Jesus said, *I saw you sitting under the fig tree.* That was the mark of a righteous man among the Hebrews.

Nathanael said, *Well, you're the Son of God,* another of the great titles for Jesus in the opening chapter of this Gospel.

When Nathanael was approached by Philip he said, *Do you mean to tell me something good can come out of Nazareth?* Look at Philip's answer to Nathanael's skepticism (John 1:46). *Come and see.* Where had he heard that? We have no better invitation to offer people than the one Jesus offered (John 1:39).

Invitation to Involvement

One of my favorite cartoons frequently depicts the circuitous journeying of one of the family's little sons. Leaving home, he pauses to take a plunge into the water sprinkler, then moves on to peek at the newest neighbor in her baby carriage. A football game with friends and a visit with a man mowing the lawn lengthen the journey, while Mother is at home wondering where her little fellow has gone.

No one would dignify this child's sojourn with the title of pilgrimage. The wanderings would classify better as meandering. Many adults, however, live their entire lives with little more direction and purpose than that found in a cartoon. Their lives are aimless; their path undetermined. Every distraction lures them away from the path. The Bible tells us they are like "infants, tossed back and forth by the waves, and blown here and there by every wind of teaching and by the cunning and craftiness of men in their deceitful scheming" (Eph. 4:14).

Just the Facts

The journey on which Christ would place our feet, however, is a pilgrimage, according to the dictionary, a journey, especially a long one, made to some sacred place as an act of devotion. The travel route is well-planned by the Father, although we can choose to detour if we like. There is a final destination, home with Him. Everything we need will be provided along the way, although we may not hold it in our hands nor see it with our eyes until needed.

The pilgrimage may take us through valleys where we must rely on our Father all the more. Every experience, however, will bring its own learning and growing. For some segments of the journey there will be no map, and we pilgrims must continue by faith. We are here for the long-haul, and with the final arrival, we will recognize it was worth the life's investment just to hear, "'Come, you who are blessed by My Father; take your inheritance, the kingdom prepared for you since the creation of the world" (Matt. 25:34). The purpose of the journey is twofold: to arrive at the destination and to make a difference along the way.

Beyond the Facts

Arriving at the destination is easy enough to understand; all God's children expect to arrive at home, greeted by the Father. But how do we make a difference along the way?

Larry Taylor has said, "Every avenue of involvement in God's mission in the world requires us to embody Christ for someone." Are others able to see Jesus in you?

In some countries in years past, elderly people for whom death seemed imminent were taken away from their homes to a place outside town. This was done so that when they died, their spirits wouldn't stay in the house. A missionary found one of these castaways and began to minister to her. Each day she brought food and drink and words of encouragement and love from Jesus. On one of the visits, the elderly woman seemed especially excited. "Jesus came to me last night," she declared, "And guess what! He looked exactly like you!"

Do others see your good works and glorify your Father in Heaven?

In Spite of the Facts

Larry Taylor has also stated, "Each mission is a calling custom-made. No two are exactly alike." Have you ever been tempted to say, "If only I could sing like her, teach like him, minister like they do, I would be faithful." If all of us, however, could only sing, who would do the preaching and teaching? How would the many physical needs of people throughout the world be met?

In Romans 12, Paul identifies some of the many gifts we have been given in our roles as Christians on pilgrimage: prophecy, exhortation, giving, leading, serving, and showing mercy and cheerfulness.

What is your role as pilgrim on the journey? Have you identified your gifts for service? If not, seek help from your pastor or a trusted Christian friend in discovering your spiritual gifts. Then commit the gifts and talents to Him for His use. The invitation to involvement is yours—personal and tailor-made. Reflect on how God has already invited you to the journey. How have you been involved in God's mission? Record your reflections.

Have there been times you stayed put, refusing to journey with God? Why? What were the results of your refusal?

Are you ready to join in the journey? Pray that He will equip you for the pilgrimage ahead.

[1]Raymond E. Brown, *The Gospel According to John (1-12),* vol. 29 of *The Anchor Bible* (Garden City, NY: Doubleday and Co., Inc.), 58-63.

[2]Ibid., 63-64.

[3]Ibid., 510-11.

[4]Alan Jones, *Passion for Pilgrimage* (New York: Harper and Row, 1989), 79.

[5]W. H. Auden, "For the Time Being," in *Collected Poems,* ed. Edward Mendelson (New York: Random House, Inc., 1976), 285-86.

[6]David Buttrick, Seventh Annual Florida Winter Pastor's School lecture, Stetson University, Deland, FL, February 1991.

[7]T. S. Eliot, "Little Gidding," in *The New Oxford Book of English Verse,* ed. Helen Gardner (New York: Oxford University Press, 1972), 897.

14

Involved with Bread and Life

Focal passage: John 6:1-35
Focal verse: John 6:35

In the Gospel of John, Jesus is the Master Teacher and He does His teaching by show-and-tell. Jesus would show by example or by miracle, and the miracles in the Gospel of John are called signs. Then He would tell by following up the sign with a discourse, an explanation.

In the synoptic Gospels (Matthew, Mark, and Luke) Jesus performs miracles, or wonders, and He teaches in parables. But John has no parables. The parables are replaced by the discourses and the miracles are replaced by the signs. In the Gospel of John there are seven signs and in chapter 6 we have two of them.

The background for John's use of signs seems to be the Exodus story. In the Exodus account God multiplied signs through Moses, yet the people still refused to believe. This pattern is reproduced in the Gospel of John. Jesus performed seven signs and still not everyone could see and believe.

John has this unusual interest in the Exodus and he has frequent references to Moses and the events of the Exodus. In chapter 6 all of that comes into focus. At the end of chapter 5 (vv. 45,46) are two references to Moses. So already John tips us off as we go into chapter 6 that he has Moses in mind.

This sixth chapter falls into three sections. The first section has to do with the feeding of the 5,000. The second section has to do with the crossing of the sea and Jesus' walking on the water. The third section is the great discourse on the Bread of life.

John skillfully sets up a contrast between Moses and Jesus. In the opening paragraph the setting is the Sea of Galilee (John 6:1). Jesus is by the sea. Moses was associated with another body of water—the Red Sea, or the Sea of Reeds. A multitude followed Jesus (John 6:2). Moses was also followed by a great multitude as he and the children of Israel left Egypt. The multitude followed Jesus (John 6:2) because of the signs that He did. Moses also performed many signs before Pharaoh. "Jesus went up on a mountainside" (John 6:3). Moses also went up into the mountain.

The setting is much like Matthew's setting of the Sermon on the Mount, except in the Gospel of Matthew, Jesus is presented as a second Moses. That's not what happens in the Gospel of John. In the Gospel of John the point is the contrast between the two. John is getting ready to offer a contrast between Moses and Jesus. It's not that Jesus is just another Moses, but Jesus is One far greater than Moses.

If there were any doubt left about the contrast John is setting up between Jesus and Moses, read verse 4. In verse 4 it's mentioned that it was the season of Passover. Who presided over the original Passover? Moses. Furthermore, the Messiah was expected at Passover. The Jewish people believed when Messiah came, He would come at Passover. All this symbolism is built into the opening verses of chapter 6, where John has skillfully set up this contrast between Moses and Jesus.

Feeding the 5,000

Jesus put His disciples to the test. "When Jesus looked up and saw a great crowd coming toward him, he said to Philip, 'Where shall we buy bread for these people to eat?' He asked this only to test him, for he already had in mind what he was going to do" (John 6:5-6). Jesus was testing His disciples. He does that still.

Why was He testing Philip? Progress, maybe. *Philip, have you made any progress since the last time we talked?*

Perhaps it was Philip's growth that Jesus tested with this question. We're not told exactly. Growth, of course, always involves change, and most of us aren't fond of changes.

Those of us who are committed to missions have no choice but to be in favor of change because we are interested in the greatest change in the world—the change in the human heart, the change in the human spirit, and the change in the human mind and the way it looks at things. It is a change so radical that we call it conversion, being born again. There is no avenue of involvement with Christ's mission apart from change. *The crowds are hungry, Philip. Something has to give, has to change. What do you propose we do about it?*

Now what answer do you suppose Jesus would liked to have received to that question? Don't you imagine it would have been music to His ears if Philip had simply said, *Lord, that's no problem with You. After all, You're the Bread of Life. We've seen the things You've done. Feeding this multitude is no problem with You.*

But Jesus seldom got that kind of perceptive, insightful response from these literal-minded disciples, who really had no taste for metaphor, and who as yet couldn't rise above whatever they could see.

Literalism can be the death of understanding, and we may be living in the most literal age in history. We think like engineers rather than poets. But, predictably enough, Philip answered Jesus' question in the usual, literal, short-sighted way.

He said, "Eight months wages would not buy enough bread for each one to have a bite!" Andrew doesn't come off much better in verse 8. He finds a young boy whose mother thought to pack a picnic lunch for him of five barley loaves and two fish. But Andrew adds woefully, *What are they among so many?* Verse 9 sets up the hopelessness, the utter impossibility of the whole situation. Jesus has posed a question to His disciples that has no answer apart from Jesus Himself. That same kind of question is programmed into your life and mine. Jesus is the only answer to the question of our lives. He always gives us the very thing He asks from us.

So Jesus had to take the situation in hand. He said, "Have the people sit down" (John 6:10). Then He took the few loaves. He didn't start from nothing. He took what was available, five loaves. Note the verbs in verse 11. He *took, gave thanks,* and *distributed.* This was the profound pattern of Jesus' activity in His ministry. He was teaching by action. This was the *show* of *show-and-tell.* He was getting ready to show this crowd what God could do with just a little bit. Jesus didn't deny people's need for daily bread. These people were hungry and poor. Some had never known what it was to have a full stomach. Gandhi said, "God Himself dare not appear to the hungry, save in the form of bread."[1]

When we show compassion and feed hungry people we then have a chance to talk to them about the Bread of life. We're following the pattern of John 6.

Bread—An Avenue for Involvement

I'm thankful for missionaries that are out there distributing food that our gifts make possible. Jesus witnessed here by a gift of food. So everybody was fed. It was probably one of the few times when their stomachs were full.

David Buttrick says, "We must preach good news once again to the poor if the church is ever going to grow."[2] This is good news to the poor. Everyone that day with his stomach full sat and watched as 12 baskets of leftovers were gathered.

Do you see what's happening? Moses provided manna in the wilderness, but just enough to get through the next day. Jesus provides enough so that everybody eats till they are full and there are 12 baskets left!

The people were so excited when they saw the sign. They responded by calling Jesus the prophet who is to come into the world. The Jews believed that in the last days another prophet like Moses would come (Deut. 18:15,18). So once again we have this parallel and contrast between Moses and the prophet like Moses. The people say, "This is the Prophet who is to come into the world" (John 6:14).

What Jesus did in feeding the 5,000 calls people to see in Him far more than just an ordinary person. This is the only one of Jesus' miracles that is recorded in all four Gospels. It later took on much greater significance in the church. Jesus feeding the people. Jesus offering bread in remembrance of Him at the Last Supper. The disciples never forgot one of the most scandalous things about Jesus was He would eat with just anybody—sinners, publicans, prostitutes, just anybody. There was a broad inclusiveness in Jesus' approach to life and to people.

So He performs this fourth sign, a bread sign. John 6:15 is transitional and the temptation is to skip right over it, but it's important: "Jesus, knowing that they intended to come and make him king by force, withdrew again to a mountain by himself." Only Jesus is perceptive. One of the ways that John describes faith in his Gospel is seeing with perception. The other two ways are believing and coming to Jesus.

But here only Jesus sees. A bread sign has been performed and nobody has seen it or understood it as yet, except Jesus. Now He perceives that the crowd is about to make Him a king. The verbs in John 6:15 are violent verbs. This crowd is about to *seize* Jesus, to *coerce* Him, *compel* Him to be their king. They've found a meal ticket. Here is a king that can feed everybody out of virtually nothing. No wonder He would make a good king in their minds. Jesus, perceiving what they were about to do to try to make Him king, withdrew.

Robert Frost wrote a poem titled, "How Hard It Is to Keep from Being King When It's in You and in the Situation." There is a character in that poem who says, "How hard it is to keep from being King when it's in you and in the situation. And that is half the trouble with the world."[3] Jesus well knew about the shortcut method to success and He avoided it.

So Jesus withdrew. Jesus could attract a crowd, but He could also leave a crowd. Unfortunately, not all of Jesus' followers have known how or when to leave a crowd, especially when a crown was in the offing. We might paraphrase Robert Frost and say, "That is half the trouble with the church."

Now that brings us to John 6:16. The context of this chapter is Passover, which recalls such things as the Exodus, the manna in the wilderness, crossing the sea, mastery over the sea, and the ability to feed the people in the wilderness. These were at the very heart of the Exodus story. Passover celebrated and remembered these things. So already the comparison and the contrast is set up between Jesus and Moses. In John 6:16-24, we have the fifth sign in the Gospel of John. Jesus walks on the water as the disciples cross the sea, immediately after He has fed the 5,000.

Do you see what's happening? The fourth sign was a bread sign. The fifth sign is a water sign. Jesus is getting ready to take His disciples safely through the waters (John 6:16). The disciples go down to the sea, get into a boat and start across the sea. Navigation is a wonderful metaphor for the Christian's experience.

"When evening came, his disciples went down to the lake, where they got into a boat and set off across the lake for Capernaum. By now it was dark, and Jesus had not yet joined them" (John 6:16-17). The winds began to rise and the seas began to billow! It was dark, and Jesus had not yet come to them. A strong wind was blowing; and when they had rowed about three or four miles, they saw Jesus walking on the sea, drawing near to the boat. They were frightened.

But He said to them, "It is I; don't be afraid" (John 6:20).

Before Jesus comes it is always dark, and the wind always blows and the seas rise. But after Jesus comes, terrified disciples hear His Word, "It is I; don't be afraid."

In the Greek text this sentence, "It is I," consists of the words *ego eimi*. It is translated, *I AM*. Does that ring any bells? From this point on in the Gospel of John, we are going to encounter I AM again and again. Seven times I AM is followed by powerful predicates. (*bread, light, way, truth, life, good shepherd, vine*).

In John 6:14 Jesus is called the "Prophet who is to come." That is a pretty lofty title. In John 6:15 the people want to make Him king. Well, He is a king, but He doesn't want to be that kind of king. King is also a pretty lofty title. But when Jesus walks on the sea, John is saying this is more than any prophet. This is more than any king. This is the divine Son of God among us. This is I AM, so named to Moses at the burning bush. The Moses-Jesus comparison continues.

Verses 22-24 of John 6 are transitional. The next day the people wake up on the grassy hillside. And guess what? Their meal ticket has disappeared and they are hungry again. So they strike out in search of Jesus.

The Bread of Life

In John 6:25, Jesus makes the transition toward the discourse on the Bread of life. This is the *tell* part of *show and tell*. He reaches out to people. Jesus offers Himself as the avenue to further involvement in His mission. Metaphor is about to become that avenue.

Jesus knew that God reaches people by means of instruction. He was the Master Teacher. He had shown them a sign. Now He's going to elaborate on it and explain it. Jesus uses people's hunger to get their attention. They could hear now that He had fed them. In the great discourse soon to follow Jesus extends to this hungry crowd the opportunity to learn.

The next morning the crowd found Jesus in the synagogue at Capernaum and they were hungry again. And when they found Him, they opened the conversation rather awkwardly. They said: *Rabbi, when did you come over here? How did you escape us? We were over on the hillside, where you spoke yesterday, and where you fed us, and we woke up and you weren't there. How did you come over here?*

Notice what they call Him in John 6:25—Rabbi. Their enthusiasm has cooled now that their stomachs are empty again. The day before when He had fed them they had called Him Prophet and they wanted to make Him king. Now He's just a rabbi again, just a teacher.

Jesus very frankly said to them, *You have sought me, not because you saw the sign. You've sought me because I fed you supper yesterday and now you expect breakfast too.*

Alan Jones says, "Not to discern the true bread is to be consumed by a useless passion for bread that leaves an aching void inside us."[4]

The crowd was back, and they were interested in bread with a small b. Jesus was ready to talk to them now about Bread with a capital B. He connected food to eternal life. (John 6:27-29). He used a pair of opposites, food which perishes and food which endures. He was getting ready to help them make the quantum leap from bread with the little *b* to

Bread with a capital *B*. It won't be easy. He uses metaphor. In metaphor we have two thoughts about different things, working together and supported by a single word. The word is *bread*. The crowd was thinking about their stomachs. Jesus was thinking about their spirits.

Since Jesus mentioned God in John 6:27, the crowd asked what they should be doing to please God. Jesus replied, there's only one work that pleases God, and that's to believe in the Christ, the One Whom God sent (John 6:29).

So, they said to Him, then what sign do you do that we may see and believe you? Did you catch the order of the verbs? *See* and *believe*. Is seeing necessarily believing? This crowd asked for a sign. They had a sign, the day before, but they hadn't really seen it.

Seeing isn't necessarily believing. One of John's favorite devices is to juxtapose seeing and believing. The Jews believed that not only would the Messiah come at Passover, but they would be able to identify Him by His ability to feed all the people. They had seen that the day before, and the comparison between Jesus and Moses goes on.

Jesus explained (John 6:32-34) it wasn't Moses that supplied the manna in the wilderness. Moses got credit for it, but God sent that little wafer in the desert every morning. God sent the Bread and now once again, says Jesus, it is God Who's giving the Bread of life.

Life is one of Jesus' favorite terms in the Gospel of John. It occurs 36 times in this Gospel. It occurs only 16 times in Matthew, Mark, and Luke put together. This is the Gospel where Jesus says, "'I am the way and the truth and the life.'"

It becomes crystal clear that the crowd is still thinking literally (John 6: 34). They aren't thinking about the Bread of life. They're thinking about what goes into their stomachs, and so they say, Lord, that's why we're here. For the bread. Just keep on feeding us this bread forever. They can't yet make the metaphorical leap beyond material bread. Jesus doesn't quit trying. He doesn't stop challenging His listeners to reach and stretch for more. As the master teacher, Jesus knew that unless He constantly demanded that His listeners stretch and reach, they'd never come up to the level of their possibilities.

Jesus pitched His message on a high level and He called on His listeners to meet Him there. We read in the Gospels that sometimes they said, *Can't you be a little more simple?* Jesus knew that simplicity has its limits. He knew that if He let people stay on a simple, easy, milk diet, they'd never grow. They'd never stretch or reach out. Bodies at rest tend to remain at rest.

James Fowler, in his ground-breaking work *Stages of Faith,* outlines six stages of faith through which we may grow and develop.[5] In this Gospel of John, much is made of the different levels of faith occupied by various people around Jesus.

Alan Culpepper, in his marvelous book *Anatomy of the Fourth Gospel,* outlines seven different faith responses in the Gospel of John. The Jews reject Jesus outright. That's the first response. People such as Nicodemus accept Jesus but without any open commitment. The lame man in chapter 5 is typical of those who accept Jesus as a worker of wonders and miracles. The Samaritan woman in chapter 4 and the blind man in chapter 9 believe in Jesus' words. They don't quite grasp it all yet, but they believe that He is telling the truth and that He is from God.

A fifth level is occupied by those who make a commitment to Jesus even though they don't understand, such as the disciples Mary and Martha. Then the sixth level has to do with model discipleship, such as the beloved disciple in the Gospel of John. He believes without seeing the resurrected Christ (John 20:8-9). And finally, there are those who come near Christ, only to fall away—the defectors, such as Judas.[6]

Jesus was a demanding teacher and His listeners didn't always catch His stories. But He kept on trying by show and tell. I remember as a college literature student reading Shakespeare and realizing that this greatest genius to use the English language composed his plays for some of the poorest, least educated, most simple people of his day. And through the play (and the play's the thing) he led them to a greater appreciation of language and life. He didn't let the intellectual paucity of his listeners hold him back.

Often there is so little in church for the mind. John Milton, the great Puritan poet, said about the pulpit in his day:

The hungry sheep look up, and are not fed,
But swollen with wind and rank mist they draw,
Rot inwardly and fowl contagion spread.[7]

"Love the Lord your God with all your heart and with all your soul and with all your mind."

Now misunderstanding, of course, took place (John 6:33-35). Misunderstanding is a common device in this Gospel. There are some 18 instances of misunderstanding, and they work like this.

First, Jesus makes a statement that is metaphorically ambiguous, maybe a statement with a double entendre. "For the bread of God is he who comes down from heaven and gives life to the world" (John 6:33).

And then, second, His conversation partner, in this case the crowd, responds literally or else asks a question, which shows they've missed the point altogether. They said to Him, Well, Lord, that's why we've come over here—for the bread. Give us this bread always.

Finally, third, an explanation or a teaching is offered by Jesus, or by the Gospel writer John, to clear it all up.[8] That's what we have in John 6:35. Jesus said to them, "I am the bread of life. He who comes to me will never go hungry, and he who believes in me will never be thirsty."

In John 6:35 we have the first of Jesus' seven "I am" sayings: "I am the bread of life." The other six are: "I am the Light of the world." "I am the gate for the sheep." "I am the good shepherd." "I am the resurrection and the life." "I am the way and the truth and the life. "I am the true vine."

By way of background consider these things: First, I AM in the Old Testament is the name of God. (Ex. 3:14). God's statement can be interpreted different ways. "'I AM that I AM.'" *You go back and tell them, Moses, that I AM has sent you.* Now what kind of name is that? What kind of an explanation is that? It could mean *I Am that I AM* or it could mean *I AM that which causes to be* or it could mean *I will be what I will be.*

The point is the mystery of God. We like things clear. We don't like any mystery in our faith. We like to have everything precise and absolute.

Occasionally we need to hear something about God, especially in church, that we don't understand. Faith grows stronger not when every i is dotted and every *t* is crossed but whenever we give ourselves to the mystery that is God. Faith without mystery and ambiguity is dead.

All seven of these predicates (vine, way, light, bread, gate for the sheep, good shepherd, and resurrection and life) are symbols either for God or for Israel in the Old Testament. They are all divine answers to human needs. Without bread, there is no life. Without light, there is no sight. Without a door, there is no exit, no entrance, and no safety. Without a shepherd, there is no guide. Without a resurrection, there is no hope. Without a way to walk, a truth to believe, and a life to live, we are lost, aimless, and confused. And without the vine, we have no substance; we have no strength.

What's Jesus saying in this passage? He's saying, *Seek what is permanent.*

T. S. Eliot wrote about our culture:

And the wind shall say: "Here were decent, godless people:
Their only monument the asphalt road
And a thousand lost golf balls."[9]

Jesus says to seek first things first. *Seek what satisfies.* The Bread of life satisfies so much that you'll never be hungry again. As the Bread of life, Jesus is both the giver and the gift. He gives the Bread that satisfies. He is the Bread that satisfies. Jesus Himself is the only answer to the petition in the Lord's Prayer, "Give us today our daily bread."

We call Him life, but live Him not. We call Him Way, but walk Him not. We call Him Truth, but believe Him not. We call Him Bread, but eat Him not. If we are lost, we can blame Him not.

Jesus spares no means to involve us with Himself and a world of hungry people. Show-and-tell, signs, discourses, metaphor, hunger, spiritual longing, appeals to history, appeals to the Scriptures. They are all here in John 6. Jesus appeals to us to spend time at His feet learning about our mission. When we've learned, when we've eaten His bread, we'll have no difficulty finding avenues for ministry to His people.

Involved with Bread and Life

Somalia 1992: No government, no food, no peace. Once again the television news subjected us to the horrors of multitudes in the feeding stations and to those unable to get to one. Bloated, distended bellies; sunken faces and haunting eyes. Flies and disease. Mothers nursing babies from empty breasts. No home, no strength, no hope.

Have you ever wondered what our spiritual bodies look like? If it were possible to see them, would they look something like those emaciated forms which haunt us on television? Would our malnourished condition mirror those pitiful bodies? Or would they, perhaps, be grossly overweight, reflecting an overabundance of spiritual food and lack of exercise?

Just the Facts

Why do you suppose Jesus used the analogy of bread as the food of the spirit? In selecting a food item to picture spiritual sustenance, Jesus didn't choose caviar, so that only the wealthy could afford it. Nor did He identify it as kimchi, for only the Koreans would have understood it. Instead He chose bread, common to all races and rank in life.

Jesus identified Himself as bread to portray His own ability to satisfy spiritual hunger, regardless of race, language, or culture. Through this metaphor, He reveals His own humanity. He has experienced physical hunger. He has felt the gnawing pangs of hunger, and He recognizes the "good news, bad news" nature of hunger. The good news is that a hearty appetite is symptom of a healthy body; the bad news is that if hunger is not satisfied, starvation will result.

What about your own appetite for spiritual nourishment? Do you long for time alone with the Father? Or do you feel glutted and sluggish with spiritual snack food? Or is it just possible that in this land of plenty you haven't availed yourself of the daily bread He wants to provide?

Beyond the Facts

Larry Taylor used the designation of the small *b* and capital *B* to distinguish between the physical bread which momentarily satisfies and the spiritual Bread which brings eternal life.

Today many people seek experiences and objects which seem for the time to be important and worthwhile. Ultimately, however, they fall into the category of things which moths and rust corrupt. The "meism" of the modern age even spills over into the religious life, causing men and women to seek churches not where they can partake of spiritual Bread but where the desires for worldly bread are met.

Larry Taylor concludes, "Jesus spares no means to involve us with Himself and a world of hungry people. . . . When we've learned, when we've eaten His bread, we'll have no difficulty finding avenues for ministry to His people." Have you fixed your appetite on the Bread Christ offers? Seek eternal nourishment through the Bread of Life, and then pass the loaf to others.

In Spite of the Facts

When the trucks loaded with food arrived in Somalia, the television cameras were there to record the distribution. Some of the people waited patiently in line, but with anguish and fear on their faces. *What if there is not enough? What if I do not get my share?*

Some grabbed and pushed in their feverish desire for supplies for themselves and their families. The overwhelming objective in their lives at that moment was to obtain food.

There are people all over the world who seek spiritual bread that only Christ can give. It is available for distribution. Can we deny them the source of life?

Reflect on what you have learned in this chapter. Are you following Jesus for the spiritual bread He provides, or for the physical bread (blessings) that may accompany being a Christian?

How is your spiritual diet? Are you starving, growing, or stuffed? Record in your journal your plan to follow a well-balanced spiritual diet, complete with Bible study, worship, prayer, ministry, and witness.

Throughout this study, you have been encouraged to meditate on people who need ministry and witness. Record what steps you have taken to introduce them to the Bread of life.

Nowhere in the Bible does Jesus say we are the bread of life. We are only the outlet through which He is presented to others. Just as the aroma of homemade bread fresh from the oven causes our mouths to water with desire, may we be the aroma of Christ, creating a hunger and thirst for Him.

[1]W. Stanley Mooneyham, *What Do You Say to a Hungry World?* (Waco: Word Books, 1975), 261.

[2]David Buttrick, Seventh Annual Florida Winter Pastor's School lecture, Stetson University, Deland, FL, February 1991.

[3]Robert Frost, "How Hard It Is to Keep from Being King When It's in You and in the Situation," in *The Poetry of Robert Frost* (New York: Holt, Rinehart, and Winston, 1969), 462.

[4]Alan Jones, *Passion for Pilgrimage* (San Francisco: Harper and Row, 1989), 181.

[5]James W.Fowler, *Stages of Faith* (San Francisco: Harper and Row, 1981).

[6]R. Alan Culpepper, *Anatomy of the Fourth Gospel* (Philadelphia: Fortress Press, 1983), 146-148.

[7]John Milton, "Lycidas," in *The Poems of John Milton,* ed. James H. Hanford (New York: Ronald Press Co., 1953), 147-48.

[8]Culpepper, *Anatomy of the Fourth Gospel,* 160-61.

[9]T. S. Eliot, "Choruses from 'The Rock,'" in *Collected Poems 1909-1935* (New York: Harcourt, Brace and Co., 1958), 190.

TEACHING GUIDE

A Note to the Teacher

This guide offers an agenda and learning activities for a 2½-hour study of *In Christ's Name*. Church Study Course credit is available for participants (see p. 155).

If you plan a shorter study, use the introductory activity, one activity from each of the four sessions, and a conclusion activity. You may wish to offer a 13-week study, in which you study one chapter per week. Since *In Christ's Name* has 14 chapters, you should omit a chapter or combine two chapters in one session. Chapters 7 and 8 may be the best ones for you to combine.

Preparation

1. Read *In Christ's Name*. Answer the reflection questions.
2. Schedule the study on the church calendar. Arrange for meeting space, nursery facilities, and publicity.
3. Arrange for simple refreshments such as coffee and soft drinks.
4. Order extra copies of *In Christ's Name*. Make them available to participants several days before the study.
5. Obtain Bibles, paper, pencils, index cards, and a flip chart or blackboard.
6. Provide the most recent edition of the newspaper, one copy for every four participants.
7. Obtain an audiocassette player and a tape of instrumental music.
8. Make all visuals.
9. Copy all learning activity handouts.
10. Make the take-home study reminders.

Remember that as the leader you are responsible for the study experience, but that does not mean you must do everything yourself. Enlisting others to help before and during the study heightens their interest and desire to attend.

Learning Climate

Make posters or banners to place around the meeting room. Choose from the following quotes.

"To choose what is difficult all one's days as if it were easy, that is faith."—W. H. Auden, poet

"In prayer it is better to have a heart without words, than words without a heart."—John Bunyan, author of *The Pilgrim's Progress*

"Grace is the incomprehensible fact that God is well pleased with a man."—Karl Barth, theologian

"Conversion is so simple that the smallest child can be converted, but it is also so profound that theologians throughout history have pondered the depth of its meaning."—Billy Graham, evangelist

"Spiritual life does not go with a secure life. You have to take risks."—Ignazio Silone, author of *Bread and Wine*

"To know God is to experience His love in Christ, and to return that love in obedience."—C. H. Dodd, theologian

DURING THE STUDY
As participants enter, distribute the Bibles, pens, paper, and index cards. Invite early arrivals to walk around the room reading the posters and banners. Have instrumental music playing softly.

Introductory Activity (10 to 15 minutes)
Tell the story of Nick (see p. 1). Ask participants the following questions, which they may wish to record on their paper.

- In your spiritual life have you had fears, as Nick had, that you are not growing the same way other people are?
- In what ways do you hope to grow spiritually in the future?
- What can you do to help yourself grow in these ways?

Ask participants to share answers if they wish to do so. You may encourage them by sharing your own answers, or ask someone ahead of time to be ready to share. Help participants feel comfortable if they choose to keep their answers private.

Learning Activities (2 hours)
Section 1: Power
1. Ask a participant to read the focal passage of chapter 1, which is Jeremiah 32:6-17. Give a brief description of Jeremiah's circumstances at the time. Ask participants to form groups of three or four (seven or eight if the group is large) and discuss the following questions: If you were in Jeremiah's position, what would have been your reaction to God's message? How would you have felt about undertaking this symbolic act?

Give the groups a 5-minute time limit for their discussion, then ask groups to report. Point out any parallels you see to Jeremiah.

Ask groups to form again and consider this question: With the world crying out for hope, what tangible act can you undertake to symbolize your faith in God's power? After 5 minutes, ask groups to report. Record their answers on the flip chart or blackboard.

2. Distribute the following handout.

> When Jesus stilled the storm, He proved His power over
>
> _____.
>
> When Jesus cast demons out of the Gadarene demoniac, He proved His power over _____.
>
> When the woman was cured by touching the hem of Jesus' robe, it proved His power over _____.
>
> When Jesus raised Jairus's daughter from the dead, He proved His power over _____.
>
> If Jesus has power over _____, _____, _____, and _____, is there anything in my life more powerful than Jesus?

Lead participants to use the handout as a listening sheet as you or a participant tells the stories from chapter 2. Ask them to answer the last question as a reflection question.

Section 2: Calling and Accountability

1. This activity compares and contrasts two biblical couples: Abraham and Sarah, and Mary and Joseph.

Divide the participants into two listening groups. One group will listen for similarities between the two couples. The other group will listen for differences between them.

Ask a participant to tell how Abraham was called and how Sarah was implicated in that call. Ask another participant to describe how Mary was called and how Joseph was implicated in that call. If you have not enlisted people beforehand, tell the stories yourself.

After the material is presented, the groups should discuss their findings. A spokesperson from each group should report.

2. Ask a participant to read the focal passage from chapter 9, which is Mark 1:16-18. Ask a participant to stand and present a case against the suitability of a tax collector and a bunch of fishermen as disciples of the gospel. Choose a person with a dramatic flair and the ability to argue.

Ask another participant to stand and make a case against the disciples following Jesus.

After the two sides are presented, share the information in chapter 9 about why Jesus calls everyone and why each of us is accountable to follow Him.

Section 3: Servanthood

1. Ask participants to stand and read the following Scripture passages. Introduce the passages by explaining that they are poems about God's ideal servant, and that scholars have long debated the identity of the servant. The passages are Isaiah 42:1-4; 49:1-6; 50:4-9; and 52:13–53:12. After the readings, explain that the next activity will show how Jesus was the New Testament fulfillment of Old Testament ideals.

2. Read this quote from Larry Taylor (p. 111). "The question of Jesus' identity over against the image of the servant is not settled by counting the number of quotes in the New Testament from Isaiah's four servant poems. It is settled best by listening to Jesus' teaching and by watching His behavior. Jesus taught service by word, deed, and being."

Using a flip chart or chalkboard, lead the group in brainstorming what the world sees as signs of greatness or importance. Then brainstorm the signs of servanthood.

Lead the discussion of these two questions: Which do you find more appealing, worldly greatness or servanthood? How did Jesus teach servanthood? Be prepared to augment the discussion with examples from chapter 12.

Section 4: Involvement

1. Read the following statement by Dellanna O'Brien (p. 133). "Arriving at the destination is easy enough to understand; all God's children expect to arrive at home, greeted by the Father. But how do we make a difference along the way?"

Ask participants to form groups of four. Distribute a newspaper to each group. Direct groups to look for articles which could lead to ways for Christians to be involved in the world's pain and need. Encourage them to look in unlikely places, such as ads, photo identification lines, even the weather report.

After 10 minutes, ask participants to give reasons not to get involved. Then ask them to sit quietly for a few moments and imagine repeating those reasons to Jesus. Ask them to imagine His response.

Conclusion (15 minutes)

Softly play the instrumental music. Invite participants to spend a few minutes reading the posters or banners around the walls. Each person should write down on an index card a quote which he or she finds particularly meaningful.

As they finish writing, remind them that this study was just an introduction to the spiritual growth principles contained in *In Christ's Name.* Encourage them to study the book individually and to complete the reflection questions.

Direct their attention to the completed activities. Ask them to reread the answers to their introductory questions. Would they change those answers now? Allow a few moments for them to record any new insights about their spiritual growth.

Remind them that Jesus has power over nature, demons, sickness, and death, as they wrote on their listening sheets. As those who have been called by Him, they have His power in their lives, and are accountable to follow Him in ministry and witness.

Ask them to look again at the newspaper. What doors of involvement are open to them in their community? In the world?

Finally, call attention to the brainstorming lists. Did they discover insights into their own desires for worldly greatness or importance?

Distribute the study reminder. As they are being distributed, ask the group to form a circle for prayer. Close with sentence prayers of thanksgiving for what God has shown each person through this study.

IN CHRIST'S NAME

. . . there is growth, like a fresh green vine.

. . . there is power, that the world cannot fathom.

. . . there is hope, springing forth ever new.

. . . there is calling, to a greater purpose.

. . . there is accountability, for faith and obedience.

. . . there is involvement, in a world of pain and joy.

. . . there is humility, like unto a servant.

. . . there is sacrifice, risk, change, and labor.

. . . there is adventure, wonder, grace, and love.

Requirements for Church Study Course Credit

In Christ's Name is course number 03-353 in the subject area Spiritual Growth and Development.

Credit for the course may be obtained in two ways: (1) conference or class—read the book and participate in a 2½-hour study; (2) individual study—read the book, do the personal learning activities, and have a church leader check written work.

Request credit on Form 725, "Church Study Course Enrollment/Credit Request" (revised), available from the Church Study Course Awards Office, 127 Ninth Avenue, North, Nashville, TN 37234.

Complete details about the Church Study Course system, courses available, and diplomas offered are in the *Church Study Course Catalog* available from the church office or Awards Office.